SYMBOLIC INTERACTIONISM
IN THE GOSPEL
ACCORDING TO JOHN

Symbolic Interactionism in the Gospel According to John

A Contextual Study on the Symbolism of Water

ELIA SHABANI MLIGO

With a Foreword by Lechion Peter Kimilike

WIPF & STOCK · Eugene, Oregon

SYMBOLIC INTERACTIONISM IN THE GOSPEL
ACCORDING TO JOHN
A Contextual Study on the Symbolism of Water

Wipf & Stock
An Imprint of Wipf and Stock Publishers
199 W. 8th Ave., Suite 3
Eugene, OR 97401

www.wipfandstock.com

ISBN 13: 978-1-62564-398-8

Manufactured in the U.S.A.

05/05/2014

Contents

Contents

Foreword

Symbolic Interactionism in the Gospel according to John: A Contextual Study on the Symbolism of Water is a book that exemplifies in detail an evolutionary sociological approach aimed at improving biblical exegesis. This book enthusiastically presents the intricacies behind the perspective of symbolic interactionism by expounding on the reality behind the symbolic act of human communication. In this way, on the one hand, the book is a unique tribute to the many scholars involved in the study of symbolic interactionism, most of whose contributions have been crucial in explicating the ideas espoused in the pages of this book. On the other hand, detailed examples and illustrations involve the reader's participation and critical thinking as a social object, as well as in a very appealing, practical way. Also, the book uses the insights of symbolic interactionism to understand dramaturgy, making the subject matter very relevant to social sciences and humanities in general. Hence, the author has managed to make a complex concept of symbolic interactionism readily accessible to the reader in simple language.

The book is divided into two main parts. The first part includes chapters 1, 2, and 3. The first part analyzes the concept of symbolic interaction as a process of actualizing the potential of perspective and language by indirectly understanding the world around us. Symbolic interaction facilitates one individual (known as the subject or self) to export his or her subjective thoughts and intentions into the public sphere of influence for others to scrutinize. In other words, whether within the self or in the other, symbolic interactionism is a communicative process that allows for open discussion in order to bring shared understanding. It does this by creating room to negotiate the meaning of a presented idea and the justification of the same between parties involved in communication. Hence, these chapters point out ways in which this process can affect our personal thinking and our subsequent behavior. As such, therefore, this part of the book brings to the fore the universal importance of the communicative function of symbols and language that is central to human life for both innovation and change. Hence, for this reason the book suggests the task of interpreters is to choose those lenses they believe to be the most helpful in approaching a given text.

The second part of the book, constituting chapter 4, focuses on the application of the method in the gospel of John. This part is the major contribution of the book to biblical studies. This informative chapter is replete with detailed examples of water symbolism in the gospel. The essence of the water symbol is verified in that it refers to reality, but it is not itself that reality. The basis for this view lies in the understanding of the perspective of symbolic interactionism expounded in the book, that the texts on water symbolism are not meant to be taken literally. For example:

- The main symbolic function of the miracle at Cana is argued to call attention to the substitution of the water prescribed for Jewish purification with wine to reveal the glory of Jesus' ability to transform things and his ability to go beyond the things of Judaism.

- The water symbolism in the story of Nicodemus is rite of passage that illustrates rebirth in faith or spirit.

- In the episode of the Samaritan woman at the well water symbolism illustrates spiritual life and eternal life, the person of Jesus himself and his offering to the world, Spirit, and knowledge of Jesus and God.

On the one hand, the key significance to this approach is the fact that in the gospel of John most of the statements mentioning water are rooted in symbolic language that develops them in a new way. In this sense it is made clear that the gospel is rich in symbolic language, water being one of them.

On the other hand, the communication act is a complex interaction of symbols and language in speech and rhetoric, setting of events, social norms, and ideologies between speaker and hearer (or in the case of a text, writer and reader). The text as a symbol is a vehicle of communication, a world unto itself, yet it represents a world outside itself that encompasses these diverse realms of communicative interactions. It is such an interaction between reader and text that is particularly important in the reading of a sacred text, which the individual and community of faith view as relevant to their lives in their setting.

Finally, it is evident that the gospel of John as a written text is not a static, objective reality; rather, it is the basis of an interaction between writer and reader. Neither is it a locus of meaning, but the focus of meaning through which the writer and reader interact. While every text is produced in a specific setting with a specific intent, the possibilities inherent in the text go beyond that original intent as the reader enters into the interpretive conversation. By using the perspective of symbolic interactionism the reader may see possibilities in the text that are valid interpretations in his or her setting, which differs significantly from the writer's intent and setting.

This book successfully provides a road map of how to channel the perspective of symbolic interactionism in biblical interpretation. I hope the author of this book is confident that there will be many grateful readers who will gain a broader perspective of the disciplines of the social sciences, and humanities in general, as a result of his efforts.

Lechion Peter Kimilike, PhD
Director of Iringa Regional Center
The Open University of Tanzania
Iringa, Tanzania
September 2013

Introduction

WE LIVE IN A world where interaction is inevitable. We interact in our own selves and with beings around us. The interaction we undergo is mainly what shapes our being and our existence in this world. This means that interaction is not contingent upon whether the person is in solitary or is in association with other beings. It is a reality of everyday life and a means through which organisms come to understand the reality around them. The interaction among human beings involves the use of existing symbols that make communication possible. Symbols are social objects that surround the human being and enable him or her to communicate the intended message, which in turn is interpreted by the receiver of that message. The communicator of the message first interprets before communicating that message or symbols to other receivers. When the person uses the symbols to communicate that message he or she does that internationally. In that case, the interaction becomes symbolic because the symbols used are used intentionally and are subject to interpretation according to contexts.

This book uses the perspective of symbolic interactionism to discuss the way characters in the gospel of John interact. The book begins by presenting what is really meant by "perspective" and why perspective is important in trying to understand the existing reality. It then discusses the perspective of symbolic interactionism and its parameters, the meaning of symbols as social objects, the origin of the perspective of symbolic interactionsm and its major proponents. I also discuss one of the model applications of symbolic interactionism: dramaturgy, as presented by Erving Goffman, who is one of the sociologists of the twentieth century. Dramaturgical representation of reality, according to Goffman, takes seriously the way characters interact when they come into immediate presence. Under this immediate presence each individual tries his or her best to influence the perception of the other individuals. In this case, the major issue in this chapter is the way each individual manages his or her impression when on the front stage.

The discussion of theoretical perspectives leads us to the use of symbolic interactionism, and the dramaturgical ideas from Goffman, to discuss the interaction of characters in the gospel according to John. The major theme of discussion is the symbolic representation of water and the way characters (actors) in the narrative scene use this symbol in the interaction order. Water is a word, and as a word it is a symbol to be defined to ascertain the meaning it carries with it. However, its meaning is contextual and specific to the particular interaction order. In this book I survey the various stages of interaction in the gospel of John and the possible meanings water stands for in such interactions. Hence since symbols stand for a certain reality, it also means that the use of water in the gospel of John also symbolically portrays a certain reality that needs to be interpreted and exemplified by readers of the gospel.

In addition to the gospel according to John, water has been used by various religions as a symbolic representation of purity and cleanliness. Moreover, in all denominations and sects of the Christian religion water is used in baptism. The use of water in the Christian religion during baptism provides a public statement that its adherents are transformed from the old lifestyle to the new one. They have received an inner cleansing of their souls. In some denominations water may be blessed by a priest and used for purification and cleansing.

In other religions such as Islam and Hinduism water is also very important for purification and the removal of what is dirty. The water of rivers is sacred in Hinduism, while Muslims wash themselves before they enter into prayers for the sake of purification. This indicates that in addition to the fact that water is a symbol of life, it is also a symbol of purification and cleanliness of the outer and inner dimensions of living beings because it washes away impurities.

ONE

The Importance of Perspective

Reality and the Question of Truth

WHY USE A PERSPECTIVE in presenting the existing reality? And what is reality so far? As David Trace maintains, "Reality is what we name our best interpretation. Truth is the reality we know through our best interpretations. Reality is constituted, not created or simply found, through the interpretations that have earned the right to be called relatively adequate or true." And what does it imply saying that reality is "constituted, not created"? This assertion most likely means that "Reality is neither out there nor in here. Reality is constituted by the interaction between a text, whether book or world, and a questioning interpreter."[1] If the above understanding of reality holds any grain of truth, this means no reality can be grasped outside the interaction between the text and the interpreter.

One response to the question regarding the use of a perspective to understand reality is that reality is vast and not easy to grasp; though, in most cases, it is taken

---

1. Tracy, *Plurality and Ambiguity*, 48.

for granted by "ordinary members of society."[2] The same reality can be grasped in a very different way in everyday life. Peter L. Berger and Thomas Luckmann write: "Every day life presents itself as a reality interpreted by men and subjectively meaningful to them as a coherent world."[3] Grasping reality is wrestling with the question of truth. The question of truth has bothered people in all times and ages. What is truth, and what is not? It is possible to hear people trying to judge something depending on how they see it. For them, and their judgment, that is their truth. In this case, truth is not universal. It is contextual and most likely individual.

This means what is seen as true to one person is not necessarily true to another, even between identical twins! Moreover, there is no single meaning of a thing, even a very small object we see with our naked eyes. Since truth or reality is not universal, and is very much dependent upon one's way of looking at things, we can simply say that truth is truth only from a particular angle and not necessarily from another angle. The angle through which we understand reality is what we can call perspective. A perspective, which is both contextual and individual, can be shared by people when they interact; and that perspective will tell us the way such people collectively view reality (truth). In this case, what is true is bound within a particular perspective, whether shared or individual.

2. Berger and Luckmann, *The Social Construction of Reality*, 19–20.

3. Ibid., 19.

Grasping Reality within a Particular Perspective

Why should we bind reality in a particular perspective and not understand it as a whole? As I said above, reality is so vast that it cannot be easily or wholly grasped. As the sociologist Joel M. Charon puts it: "Human beings always see reality through perspectives."[4] Perspectives act to us as "angles of vision" through which we see reality (or truth) around us.[5] In this case, perspectives have significant functions in our understanding of reality.

Charon lists some of the functions of perspectives in our endeavor to understand reality when he writes, "Perspectives force us to pull out certain stimuli from our environment and to totally ignore other stimuli. Perspectives force us to make sense of those stimuli in one way rather than another. Perspectives sensitize the individual to see parts of the reality, they desensitize the individual to other parts, and they guide the individual to make sense of the reality to which he or she is sensitized."[6] Charon then concludes: "Seen in this light, a perspective is an absolutely basic part of everyone's existence, and it acts as a filter through which everything around us is perceived and interpreted. There is no possible way that the individual can encounter reality 'in the raw,' directly, as it really is, for whatever is seen can be only part of the real situation."[7] In this case, we can conclude that a perspective can be known by several names: an angle of vision, an eyeglass, an individual or group's point of view, a sensitizer, or an

---

4. Charon, *Symbolic Interactionism*, 3.
5. Ibid.
6. Ibid.
7. Ibid.

individual or group's line of argument. Each of these names illuminate to us the way truth, as a stimuli from our own environments, can be grasped, filtered, and understood.

Components of a Perspective

Perspectives are made of words that make the understanding of a particular reality possible. It is a "set of interrelated words" that make it possible to understand a certain "physical reality."[8] It is a "conceptual framework," whereby concepts are interwoven to make some assumptions about what is physically seen for the purpose of trying to understand it. In this case, as Charon puts it, the understanding of reality in a particular situation depends greatly on the types of words (concepts) used in order to understand it.[9]

Words used in understanding reality form sets of ideas, sets of assumptions, and sets of values that influence our perceptions and actions. They influence what we see and the way we interpret what we see. They can also influence the way we behave in various situations. A person cannot have only one perspective in every situation. There is the possibility of having several perspectives in every situation. For example, at school I am a student; at home I am a father; at the pastors' conference I am a pastor; in the group of scholars I am an academic. I endeavor to take a perspective depending on the situation I find myself in without necessarily mixing these perspectives. This is what it means for a perspective to be contextual or situational in nature.

8. Ibid., 4.
9. Ibid.

Charon writes thus: perspectives "are our 'eyeglasses' we put on to see."[10] Being an eyeglass, each perspective contributes to the understanding of reality, not understanding the whole reality but just part of it. Someone's perspective is not something permanent; it is something eligible to change. Whenever the perspective changes it means a development of a new reality. When a person goes to school he or she acquires the perspective of a student. When a person completes schooling and is elected a leader of the community, his or her perspective changes. The perspective changes from that of a student to that of an employee. In that case, the change indicates a new reality, a new truth. Why does the truth change? The truth changes because the person secures new interactions that open up new possibilities of understanding the world around him or her.[11]

Perspectives are Asymmetrical and Subject to Change

I also remember the way my perspectives changed in the course of my educational progression. When I was in primary school my perspective and the way of understanding the world around me was different from when I attended secondary school studies. My perspective even changed as I went to an advanced level secondary school, to the university for my undergraduate studies, and to Europe for my postgraduate studies. In each case I had a particular type of interaction that shaped by perception of the world around me. The perception changed as I secured new types of interactions that exposed me to new realities. Most of

10. Ibid., 8.
11. Cf. Ibid., 6.

the past concepts I had acquired new meanings in every new interaction I engaged in.

Now let us ask: are all perspectives equal? This question is important. If all perspectives are our eyeglasses, our viewpoints, our angles of vision to view some reality, can we consider them to be equal in that manner? Perspectives are certainly not equal. There are some that bring us closer to reality than others. However, it is not easy to judge which perspective is better and which is not. There are some criteria or standards needed to measure that perspective in order to determine whether it is better than the others. In most cases, it is possible for most of us to believe that "my perspective is better than yours" in bringing us closer to the truth, except for a seriously engaged seeker of truth.[12] "A good perspective," Charon writes, "gives us insight, clearly describes reality, [and] helps us find the truth."[13] According to Charon, therefore, there is no perspective without a search for truth.

12. Ibid., 8.
13. Ibid., 9.

TWO

The Perspective of
Symbolic Interactionism

*Symbols are as important to us as is water to fish.
Without symbols we simply cannot converse with one
another. In fact, we are in chaos!*

—GERALD ARBUCKLE, *CULTURE, INCULTURATION,
AND THEOLOGIANS*

Introduction

HAVING DEFINED PERSPECTIVE AND described its importance in approaching a particular truth, let us now have a close look at one of such perspectives: the perspective of symbolic interactionism as proposed by some North American sociologists. In fact, as Arbuckle points it out: "Symbols are as important to us as is water to fish. Without symbols we simply cannot converse with one another. In fact, we are in chaos!"[1] This means no plausible communication can be attained in any scene and eventually no

1. Arbuckle, *Culture, Inculturation and Theologians*, 19.

plausible interaction can be possible without the use of symbols.

In this chapter, we will examine the background of this perspective, the three main assumptions of this perspective, the role of the individual person in the production of an action, the importance of symbols, and the perspective of symbolic interactionism as an eye for viewing reality. Hence, the discussion of the perspective of symbolic interactionism will lead to discussing the dramaturgy as presented by one of its proponents—Erving Goffman.

Background of the Perspective

Perhaps the most important and enduring sociological perspective from North America has been symbolic interactionism. Its roots are traced back to the pragmatist philosophers such as Charles Peirce, John Dewey, Charles Cooley, and George Herbert Mead of the late nineteenth century and early twentieth century.[2] Some of the sociologists who developed and continued to use this perspective include Herbert Blumer, Howard Becker, Erving Goffman, Norman Denzin, Tomatsu Shibutani, and Spencer Cahil. Some of the characteristics of the symbolic interactionist perspective are an emphasis on interactions among people, use of symbols in communication and interaction, interpretation as part of action, self as constructed by others through communication and interaction, and flexible, adjustable social processes. Its main concern tends to be the interaction order of daily life and experiences, rather than the structures associated with large-scale and relatively fixed social forces and laws. In this case, symbolic

2. Blumer, *Symbolic Interactionism*, 1; Charon, *Symbolic Interactionism*, 29.

interactionism is a point of view, or an angle through which we can view the interaction of people in their daily lives and experiences.

While the symbolic interactionist perspective is sometimes associated with Mead (ca. 1863–1931), it was Herbert Blumer (1900–1987) who took Mead's ideas and developed them into a more systematic sociological approach. Blumer coined the term "symbolic interactionism" in 1937, keeping this sociological perspective alive through the early 1950s in Chicago, and then in California where he was a professor at the University of California in Berkeley. While Holton and Cohen argue that Blumer took only certain ideas from Mead, it was the specific aspects developed by Blumer that formed the basis for later symbolic interactionist approaches. Blumer thus notes:

> The term "symbolic interaction" refers, of course, to the peculiar and distinctive character of interaction as it takes place between human beings. The peculiarity consists in the fact that human beings interpret or "define" each other's actions instead of merely reacting to each other's actions. Their "response" is not made directly to the actions of one another but instead is based on the meaning which they attach to such actions. Thus, human interaction is mediated by the use of symbols, by interpretation, or by ascertaining the meaning of one another's actions. This mediation is equivalent to inserting a process of interpretation between stimulus and response in the case of human behavior.[3]

This definition describes why the perspective is called symbolic interactionism. It is stated that the major component that characterizes human interaction is the use

3. Blumer, *Symbolic Interactionism*, 78–79.

of symbols, which are interpreted by the interacting individuals in order to enhance communication. Joel M. Charon makes Blumer's above definition more clear. He writes that symbolic interactionism is *"the study of human beings interacting symbolically with one another and with themselves, and in the process of that symbolic interaction making decisions and directing their streams of action."*[4] Charon further notes: "When we say that social interaction is symbolic, we mean that the acts of each actor have meaning to the actor doing them and are acts normally interpreted by those with whom the actor acts toward."[5] However, this does not deny the fact that the actor first acts inwardly (covert action) before acting to others, and this does not guarantee the actor's meaning will be interpreted as intended. This means that actions as symbols are free of interpretation and carry with them abundant meaning.

Three Main Premises of This Perspective

Every perspective has its philosophical standpoints that characterize its major claims for truth. This is also the case for symbolic interactionism. According to Blumer, the characteristics of this approach are the following: (1) human interaction, (2) interpretation or definition rather than mere reaction, (3) response based on meaning, (4) use of symbols, (5) and interpretation between stimulus and response.[6] Blumer proposed three main premises that underlie the whole process of symbolic interaction:

4. Charon, *Symbolic Interactionism*, 151 (emphasis is in original).

5. Ibid.

6. Blumer, *Symbolic Interactionism*, 2.

The first premise is that human beings act toward things on the basis of the meanings that
the things have for them. Such things include
everything that the human being may note in
his [or her] world—physical objects, such as
trees or chairs; other human beings, such as a
mother or a store clerk; categories of human beings, such as friends or enemies; institutions, as
a school or government; guiding ideas, such as
individual independence or honesty; activities
of others, such as their command or requests;
and such situations as an individual encounters
in his [or her] daily life.[7]

According to the above premise, what we see is not real. It
is just a product of our interpretation. A book is a book because one has interpreted it to be a book. The materials that
make a book have been interpreted to carry that meaning
in that particular context. However, what is called a book
may not mean the same thing in all places. This is really
what is meant by the contextual nature of symbols used
in interaction, as it will be seen in the following sections.

"The second premise is that the meaning of such
things is derived from, or arises out of, the social interaction that one has with one's fellows."[8] What Blumer emphasizes in this premise is that acts and their interpretations
entail the process of communication. Actions are kinds of
languages used to communicate. When a child is punished
for disobeying his parents the punishment is a kind of language communicating the bad actions of the child. In turn
the act of disobedience done by the child is also a language
communicated to the mother and father. In this case both

7. Ibid.
8. Ibid.

parties have engaged in an interaction by the use of the above-mentioned symbols.

"The third premise is that these meanings are handled in, and modified through, an interpretative process used by the person in dealing with the things he [or she] encounters."[9] This third premise promises that the interaction between two or more individuals is systematic and orderly. The meaning carried by every symbol is handled through the process of interpretation whereby it is modified according to the encounters of individuals. This means the same symbol can have several meanings depending on the encounters of the individual. In this case, the interacting individuals always struggle to interpret symbols surrounding them.

These three core premises deal with *meaning, language*, and *thought*; the three premises show that all social interactions involve *meanings* and *interpretations*, and the interactionist perspective highlights the way in which the social world is actively constructed rather than passively experienced. In the following few paragraphs I will discuss each of these ideas, which are the center of the above three premises.

Meaning

Now I discuss the two aspects that are very central to the first premise: the nature of social interaction itself and the nature of objects used in interaction.

9. Ibid.

Nature of Social Interaction

Charon notes that the symbolic interactionist perspective is not just concerned with the individual and his or her personality, or with society and the way it can enhance human behavior, but with the nature of social interactions among people who are involved in the interaction process.[10] Actions are not only individual actions, nor are they actions with personal meaning. Rather, actions are always joined with the mutual response and adjustment of the actors in the interaction process.[11] The self is one which emerges not just from the individual, but from how others see him or her, and how this person responds to and develops his or her own responses to this. Humans act according to the acts of others; they take into accounts the acts of other people. This means the acts of actors are not the same everywhere and at all times, but they change according to situations and types of actors the acting individual is involved with.

During the interaction process, actors influence one another and hence make everyone among the actors align his or her acts depending on the influence received from the other actors surrounding him or her. As Charon states:

> Interaction means that the acts of each individual are built up over time depending in part on what others do in the situation. Interaction means that individuals are not simply influenced by others; it means that actors consistently influence one another as they act back and forth;

10. Charon, *Symbolic Interactionism*, 27.

11. The word "adjustment" means each actor adjusting his or her acts in relation to the action of the other actor. "Adjusting acts in relation to one another involves understanding the actions from the perspective of the other," (Charon, *Symbolic Interactionism*, 153).

> hence, a more dynamic and active human being
> emerges, rather than an actor merely respond-
> ing to others in the environment.[12]

This way of acting back and forth among actors makes interaction an ongoing process, a process central to everything done by actors in a particular society. It becomes a social interaction.

What is social interaction? In order to understand what social interaction means, we first need to understand what a social action is. Charon writes that "When we interact we become social *objects to one another*; we use symbols; we direct self, engage in mind/covert action, make decisions, change directions, share perspectives, define reality, define the situation, and role take."[13] According to Charon, a person needs to understand these activities in order to understand the nature of interaction that exists among individuals. A social action considers most of the above aspects, especially considering that individuals are social objects to one another.

In most cases, the act uses other individuals as social objects to understand reality. Charon gives some examples of what I can do as I use other individuals as social objects: "I talk to you, listen to you, wink at you, ignore you, impress you, make love to you, greet you—in all these ways and many others I am engaging in social action because you are a social object to me in the situation."[14] What Charon says here is that the action is social action when "what the actor does involves another person or persons."[15] The actor takes the other individual into account. What

12. Ibid., 23.
13. Ibid., 149 (emphasis added).
14. Ibid.
15. Ibid.

the actor does in a particular situation depends very much
on that situation and is guided by it. This is what it means
by other people being social objects of the actor: they are
important for the actor's action and they guide what the
actor does. Charon emphasizes that the social action is
symbolic in nature because the action of the actor represents a certain meaning and intends to communicate that
meaning to other individuals.

Interaction, therefore, has its foundation in social action. It means "*actors take one another into account, communicate, and interpret one another as they go along.* . . . I
act; you consider my act, and you act; I consider your act,
and I act; you consider my act, and you act. This give-and-
take process is what is meant by interaction."[16] Interaction
is spontaneous and situational. It is not predetermined.
One cannot know how he or she will act in a short time to
come. The actor's action depends on the other individuals who are social objects to him or her, and guide his/her
action.[17] Since interaction involves actors taking one another into account, communicating and interpreting one
another's actions, and that actions provided by the acting
individuals are symbolic in nature, then social interaction
is action that is symbolic in nature and requires "continuously *taking the role of the other.*"[18] Hence, we can now understand that in most cases social interaction is symbolic
because it involves the actors' interpreting each others' acts
that represent them (see the definition of symbolic interactionism earlier).

Social interaction, as symbolic interaction, takes
two forms or levels, according to Herbert Mead: "'the

16. Ibid., 150.
17. Ibid., 150–51.
18. Ibid., 151.

15

conversation of gestures' and 'the use of significant symbols.'"[19] Blumer calls such levels of interaction as "non-symbolic" and "symbolic interaction" respectively.[20] According to Blumer, "Non-symbolic interaction takes place when one responds directly to the action of another without interpreting that action; symbolic interaction involves interpretation of the action."[21] Blumer asserts that non-symbolic interactions are common in reflex actions whereby the individual responds immediately to the situation facing him or her, for example, responding to one's bodily movement, to one's tones of voice, to hazards facing him or her, etc.

In order for the interaction to proceed, actors have to make indications to each other. Individuals have to indicate to others how to act and also respond to the indications of others. In this case

> The central place and importance of symbolic interaction in human group life and conduct should be apparent. A human society or group consists of people in association. Such association exists necessarily in the form of people acting toward one another and thus engaging in social interaction. Such interaction in human society is characteristically and predominantly on the symbolic level; as individuals acting individually, collectively or as agents of some organization encounter one another, they are necessarily required to take account of the actions of one another as they form their own action. They do this by a dual process of indicating

19. Blumer, *Symbolic Interactionism*, 8.
20. Ibid.
21. Ibid.

to others how to act and interpreting the indications made by others.

Charon concludes that "Social interaction is . . . accompa-
nied by all kinds of covert interaction, including taking the
role of the other, thinking about one's own communication, interpreting the acts of others, and considering both
the expectations and the directions of others."[22]

The Nature of Objects

Turning to the nature of objects, we observe that the
human being, as a social object, is different from other
organisms in the sense that he or she can define the surrounding situation. A human being cannot only sense the
situation, but also provides meaning to that situation. "I
do not, therefore, respond to you, to your words, to your
acts, to your clothes; instead, I define those objects in my
situation and I act according to whatever definition I have
given them at the time."[23] This is what mostly Blumer
means when he says: "The symbolic interactionists view
social interaction as primarily a communicative process
in which . . . a person responds not to what another individual says or does, but to the meaning of what he says
or does."[24] In social interaction individuals respond to the
meaning of objects around them. Definitions provided to
the surrounding objects help the individual act accordingly. Reality can exist somewhere, and the same reality can
have different meanings for every individual depending
on the objects that the individual interprets. Since reality

22. Charon, *Symbolic Interactionism*, 153.
23. Ibid., 28.
24. Blumer, *George Herbert Mead*, xii.

has a different meaning for every individual depending on the objects under interpretation, the same reality can make individuals act differently in response to the meaning they have made from that reality. In this case, "what we do does not result simply from reality as it is but from how we define what it is."[25]

What, then, is an object according to symbolic interactionism? According to symbolic interactionism, "An object is anything that can be indicated, anything that is pointed to or referred to."[26] In symbolic interactionism, objects can be singled out in three main groups: "(a) physical objects, such as chairs, trees or bicycles; (b) social objects, such as students, priests, a president, a mother, or a friend; and (c) abstract objects, such as moral principles, philosophical doctrines, or ideas such as justice, exploitation, compassion."[27]

According to Charon and Blumer, all objects are mostly social objects. This is because, according to them, a human being can see an object in a certain perspective, the perspective of the society. This means that even though the object is physical, social, or abstract, as pointed out earlier, it is yet understood within a fabric of a particular society. What then is a social object according to Blumer and Charon? According to Charon, "A social object is any object in a situation that an actor uses in that situation. That use has arisen socially. That use is understood and can be applied to a variety of situations."[28] Charon provides the following examples of social objects:

25. Charon, *Symbolic Interactionism*, 28.

26. Blumer, *Symbolic Interactionism*, 10.

27. Ibid., 10–11.

28. Charon, *Symbolic Interactionism*, 46.

1. Physical natural objects—a tree, a flower, a rock, or dirt . . .

2. Human-made objects—a radio, a fork, a piece of paper, a computer terminal . . .

3. Animals are sometimes used as social objects by the individual.

4. Other people are social objects. Both individually and in groups, we define other people as important to the situations we are in. We develop lines of actions towards them, and we "use" them . . .

5. Our "past" is a social object as is the "future." We use these to work through situations.

6. Our "self" is a social object . . .

7. Symbols are social objects. We create and use symbols to communicate and represent something to others and to ourselves.

8. Ideas and perspectives can be social objects.

9. Emotions can be social objects. As with everything else, we can define, use, manipulate, and understand emotions in ourselves and in others.[29]

Blumer emphasizes that "all objects are social products, in the vital sense that the meaning that gives each one of the objects its particular character emerges out of the process of interaction between people."[30]

---

29. Ibid.
30. Blumer, *George Herbert Mead*, 47.

Language

The previous section embarked on a discussion about meaning as embodied in social interactions and social objects. This section deals with language as an important symbol for drawing meaning from social objects and social interactions. To say meaning arises out of the interacting people means it is not pre-existent in the objects in the state of nature, nor is it inherent in the objects. Meaning is created, negotiated in everyday life through people's *use of language*. Berger and Luckmann make this clearer: "The language used in every day life continuously provides me with the necessary objectifications and posits the order within which these make sense and within which every day life has meaning for me."[31] Language is itself a great symbol, hence, the name symbolic interactionism. The use of language enables human beings *to name* surrounding objects according to their wishes or according to their agreement. The name provided sounds like the object it represents. It is only by naming objects in order to enhance communication that symbolic interaction emerges. Symbols or names are arbitrary representations of a certain meaning; the meaning is not inherent in the objects.

Symbolic interactionism believes that naming in order to enhance communication is the basis of any human society. What was the first task of Adam as described by the book of Genesis? His first task in the formation of society, according to the book of Genesis, was *to name* the animals (objects) around him. It means that nothing can be known unless it is defined and named. We know objects through the names provided to them. In this case, names carry meaning in them.

31. Berger and Luckmann, *The Social Construction of Reality*, 22.

The process of giving names to the phenomena we classify (i.e., labeling) is significant because the names or labels we create (e.g., father, criminal, insane, righteous, rich, poor, carpenter, driver, and the like) help us to define (or stereotype) the nature of the social categories we create within our society. In modern societies people tend to behave towards each other on the basis of the labels or names that each person attracts from others. The processes of naming and categorization of social categories in society is possible through the use of symbols. I briefly discuss the meaning and use of symbols in human interaction below.

Symbols Are Social Objects

The most interesting question regarding symbols as social objects concerns their meaning. What is a symbol? In symbolic interactionism, social objects are used and defined by the individuals in their process of using them. "*Symbols are social objects used to represent (or stand for, 'take the place of') whatever people agree they shall represent.*"[32] For example, for Christians the cross drawn or wooden represents the suffering of Jesus and the source of their salvation; a fish drawn represents Jesus Christ as the savior and Son of God; the nodding of heads represent accepting an idea or teaching; the word "woman" represents one gender of humanity. This means symbols are objects agreed to be used in communication and have meaning in them.

Words Spoken or Written Are Symbols

Words written and verbally spoken are also symbols representing some tangible things or situations. Real things

32. Charon, *Symbolic Interactionism*, 46 (emphasis original).

themselves are symbols to represent what we understand from our definitions of that real thing. For English speakers, the word "table" made by five letters is a symbol to represent something made of wood, or something we put food on during dining time, or something we write on. All these are represented by the word "table." Every language has its own word or words to represent the thing stated. The Swahili language for example has the word "meza" instead of the word "table" used in English. In this case, every word spoken or written is an arbitrary symbol representing something according to the way people have agreed it should; and every real thing represented by words or word is also a symbol to be defined.

Em Griffin writes thus about words as arbitrary symbols: "Because words are arbitrary symbols, they have no inherent meaning. Like chameleons that take on the coloration of their environment, words . . . take on the meaning of the context in which a person encounters them. This suggests that 'most words, as they pass from context to context, change their meaning.'"[33] The word 'context' here does not only mean that the other words in the same sentence or phrases are adjacent to the word; context is more than that. It means a "cluster of events that occur together."[34] According to Griffin, to say the context is "a cluster of events" appearing simultaneously within a particular situation "means that context is not just a sentence or even a situation in which the word is spoken. Context is the whole field of experience that can be connected with the event—including thoughts of similar events."[35]

33. Griffin, *A First Look*, 58.
34. Ibid.
35. Ibid.

Symbols Represent Meaning and Are Used to Communicate That Meaning

As I have just said above, the main role of symbols is to represent what people want them to represent. A picture of a heart can represent love; an arm raised with a fist may represent victory or readiness to fight; smiling may represent happiness or love, etc. As Charon thus writes, "Symbols represent, but they are also used for communication between actors or within the actor. Symbols are therefore *social objects used by the actor for representation and communication*."[36] Symbols enable us to inform other people what we think; they enable us to communicate what we feel, to communicate what we plan to do, and to also communicate to ourselves what we plan and what we think about our surrounding world. The word "pig" is a symbol I use to communicate to myself and to other people about a certain animal. The word "shirt" is used when I communicate to others and to myself about a certain piece of cloth. The word "cold" is a word used to communicate to myself and to others about a certain type of weather, etc. In this case, symbols are used to communicate our feelings, our plans, and our information to others and to ourselves.

However, "Not all meanings of symbols are accessible, because they lie unarticulated, perhaps mostly unexamined in the innermost corners of people's minds; anthropologists variously call them 'unconscious,' 'tacit,' or 'implicit.'"[37] This inaccessibility of all meanings within a particular symbol possibly means that only the interpreter's interpretation is the real interpretation of the symbol.

36. Charon, *Symbolic Interactionism*, 47 (emphasis original).
37. Arbuckle, *Inculturation and Theologians*, 28.

Symbols Need to Be Interpreted in Order For Us to Understand Their Meaning

In his book *Symbolic Construction of Community*, Anthony P. Cohen writes thus: "Learning words, acquiring the components of language, gives you the capacity to communicate with other people, but does not tell you *what* to communicate. Similarly with symbols: they do not tell us *what* to mean, but give us the capacity to make meaning."[38] This means, as pointed out in the preceding paragraph, symbols, as means of communication, need to be interpreted and understood. "Understanding symbols means that we understand their representation."[39] Understanding the meaning of a particular symbol is not just by training and memorizing, but by one's own will and by one's own interpretation of that symbol. In this way, symbols, as social objects, are social, meaningful, and significant. However, the meaning a particular symbol carries with it is not necessarily the same to all interpreters. Arbuckle states this more clearly when he writes: "The interpretations we give to symbols are 'ours' because they may not fit the meanings intended by the people we are observing."[40] In this case, symbols carry with them an abundance of meanings whose number is as great as those who endeavor to interpret that symbol.

As we have just said above, meaning is determined by the interpreter according to his or her own perception and the context at which that interpreter is located. This is most likely what Arbuckle points out when he states: "As symbols are cultural constructs, it is rare that any symbol is

38. Cohen, *Symbolic Construction*, 16 (emphasis is in original).
39. Ibid., 47.
40. Arbuckle, *Inculturation and Theologians*, 28.

able to have a universally recognized meaning."[41] According to Arbuckle's statement, meaning resides to the one interpreting the symbol, not to the majority understanding of the symbol. However, the agreed meaning can enhance communication and interaction but this might not be the one held by all members of a particular society.

Symbols Are Created by Human Beings

Saying that symbols are social objects means that they do not just happen spontaneously. Arbuckle clearly notes: "Symbols with their variety of meanings are born because they respond to the subjective needs of people and their experience of life."[42] Arbuckle's statement above implies that people in the society "make them, and people agree on what they shall stand for."[43] In that understanding, symbols may be conventional or not conventional. By being conventional, symbols may be seen to represent something only because of "common agreement" and may have other representations that are not agreed upon.[44]

Saying that symbols are meaningful implies they carry meaning with them. The use of a particular symbol understands its meaning (i.e., communicates the meaning of that symbol) to him or herself first before communicating that meaning to other people. Charon asserts that "Symbols involve an understanding rather than simply responding to their presence. When we say that symbols 'represent' something to the user, we are actually saying that they stand in for something else and that the user

41. Ibid., 27.
42. Ibid., 29.
43. Charon, *Symbolic Interactionism*, 47.
44. Ibid.

understands that relationship."[45] Charon quotes Tomatsu Shibutani to show what a piece of cloth called a "flag" as a symbol may represent:

> A flag is a symbol for a nation. The piece of co-
> loured cloth often evokes patriotic sentiments
> and plays an important part in the mobilization
> of millions of men for war. Seeing someone treat
> the flag with disrespect can arose the most vio-
> lent emotional reactions, for [men] often regard
> the piece of cloth as if it were the nation with
> which they identify themselves. . . . Soldiers
> risk their lives on battlefields to save a flag from
> falling into the hands of the enemy; the cloth in
> itself is of little value, but what it stands for is of
> great importance.[46]

This statement shows how important a symbol is as a social object that has meaning and is used by the society to
represent something more important than the material
used to make that symbol.

Symbols Have Meanings to Both User and the Other

The symbol is meaningful, not only to the one to whom
the meaning is communicated, but also to the one who
uses the symbol to communicate the message. The symbol
communicates a message not only to those receiving it,
but also internally. This is because the one using the symbol to communicate meaning to others does not do that
spontaneously but intentionally. A good example is a crying infant. It is possible the infant can unintentionally cry.
This crying communicates meaning to the mother, who

45. Ibid., 47.
46. Ibid., 48.

interprets the meaning and acts according to the meaning obtained. The crying of the infant becomes a social object to the mother who provides meaning to the crying infant. It is not a symbol to the crying infant, because it was not intentional and was not communicated to itself. This means the infant did not use any symbol to communicate meaning to its mother, and neither did it understand the act of its mother. If the infant intentionally cries in order to provide certain meaning to its mother, then that becomes a symbol to the infant. The infant uses that symbol to communicate meaning, both to itself and to its mother. The mother interprets the communicated meaning and acts accordingly, and the infant in turn interprets the acts of the mother. Therefore, the crying of the infant becomes a symbol for the infant to communicate meaning. In this case, crying stands for something significant that both the infant's self and the mother needs to understand.

Symbolic interactionism contends that for the act to be symbolic, symbols should communicate meaning to both the actor (the user of symbol) and the other (the one that receives the meaning). Charon thus writes, "It is important to realize that symbolic communication can actually take two forms: In one, an actor can use symbols to talk to self (think); in another, an actor can use symbols to communicate to others. However, for communication to be symbolic in the second sense (in communicating with others), the actor simultaneously talks to self (the actor understands the meaning of his or her act)."[47] According to Charon, "A symbol, then, is a *social object* used for *communication to self* or *for communication to others and to self*. It is an object used to *represent* something else. It is *intentionally* used. The actor's aim is to use it. Without

47. Ibid., 48–49.

intention, the actor may be communicating, but we do not call it symbolic."[48]

Following the above conclusion, we can say that all symbols are social objects, yet not all social objects are symbols. While all social objects can be defined according to their use, not all social objects are symbols in virtue of their capability to be defined. Hence, symbols are symbols only in virtue of their use in representation and communication.

Language Is the Core Vehicle of the Use of Symbols

Language is made up of words (symbols). Since language is made up of symbols (words), it is itself a symbol. Charon puts it this way, "Language is a special kind of symbol. More than any other symbol, it can be produced at will, and it can represent a reality that other symbols cannot. . . . Language is a set of words used for communication and representation. Words—symbols that are spoken or written—are the basis for all other symbols."[49] James A. Herrick sees language to be a symbol that belongs to symbol systems. He writes:

> Language is a symbol system using written and spoken words to communicate meaning. Music also is a symbol system, one that employs notes, markings, sound, and rhythm to communicate meaning. The movements in dance are a set of symbols enabling meaning to be expressed, as are the gestures, postures, and expressions by which we communicate without speaking. In cinema, camera angles, spatial relationships,

48. Ibid., 49 (emphasis original).
49. Ibid., 51.

and lighting can be symbolic, as can the form,
line, and colour in painting. Similarly, the lines,
shapes, and materials used in architecture are
symbols that can be used to communicate
meaning.[50]

Why are words used in language the basis of all
symbols? This is certainly because words enable us to understand the social objects surrounding us. Words used in
language are meant to represent and communicate. They
represent physical, ideological, emotional, or conceptual
reality. Through words, that make a language, we can understand other symbols. We can conclude that "Words,
then are not simply one kind of symbol but are, in fact, the
most important kind and make possible all others."[51]

The Use of Symbols Helps Distinguish between Symbolic and Non-Symbolic Interaction

How can we distinguish between symbolic and non-symbolic communications? Charon writes thus: "It is easier to
understand what is and is not a symbol from the standpoint of the one who gives it off. Simply put: It is a symbol
if an individual uses it intentionally to communicate and
represent."[52] What Charon means in this statement is that
communication becomes symbolic if the actor uses a symbol intentionally to communicate meaning, and also interprets the acts of people to whom he or she communicates
such meaning. Charon then emphasizes, "All of your acts
that I interpret are actually social objects to me. I use them
to understand you. They are not, however, symbols to me,

50. Herrick, *The History and Theory*, 5–6.
51. Charon, *Symbolic Interactionism*, 51.
52. Ibid., 50.

because I am not using them for communication and representation. To be a symbol, an action must have meaning to the actor who performs it. As he or she communicates to others, he or she understands the action."[53] In this case, the distinction between symbolic and non-symbolic communication becomes clear: what is given out (by the actor) is used by other people. This can be just a social object (if it does not intend to represent and communicate meaning) or a symbol (if it is used intentionally to communicate meaning).

Thought or Thinking

After discussing language as an important symbol used to understand other symbols, we now turn to thinking or thought as an interaction within the individual. According to Charon, "Human action is caused not only by interaction between individuals but also by interaction within the individual."[54] Charon's statement means that the action of the individual is the product of thinking (covert action). A person acts depending solely on how he or she thinks in a particular situation, certainly being influenced by the ongoing interaction with other actors.[55]

To say that the individual's interpretation of the social objects around him/her is modified by his/her thought is to say that an individual (human being) has the capacity to think. Thinking means holding an inner conversation within the individual. It is "minding," in the language of George Herbert Mead, where an individual holds a dialogue with him or herself. Let us now consider in more

53. Ibid.
54. Ibid., 27.
55. Ibid.

detail the two concepts relating to one's interaction within the self: mind action and the self.

The Mind Action

Charon calls the ability to think as "mind action," that is, the ability of a human being to make indications towards the self, to control overt actions, solve problems and control the whole interaction. To make indications towards the self, as I have just said, is to have inner dialogue within the individual. By definition, "Mind is all the action that the actor takes towards himself or herself. It is all thinking, all active manipulation of symbols by the actor in conversation within his [or her] head and towards self."[56] Self-indication is a continuous process: from the time the individual gets up in the morning to the time he or she falls asleep. In whatever we physically act, we have to have a dialogue with the self before we implement it. We make plans of action for the objects around us before we can use them for our purpose. As Charon says, "Mind [or thinking] means telling ourselves what exists around us, and, because we understand these things, we are able to determine how we are going to use them."[57] This means the meaning of our actions emanates from our inner dialogue trying to interpret and re-interpret the surrounding objects within ourselves; and what we act is just a result of our own thinking and understanding of those objects.

In fact, to control overt actions is to respond to the stimuli in our environment. We respond to the objects around us by indicating them to us and defining them into

56. Ibid., 98.
57. Ibid., 99.

our minds what they mean. Charon, quoting Blumer provides the meaning of indication thus:

> To indicate something is to stand over against it and to put oneself in the position of acting toward it instead of automatically responding to it. In the face of something which one indicates, one can withhold action toward it, inspect it, judge it, ascertain its meaning, determine its possibilities, and direct one's action with regard to it. With the mechanism of self-indication the human being ceases to be a responding organism whose behavior is a product of what plays upon [him or her] from outside, the inside, or both.[58]

In this case, the mind, or the ability to think, enables him or her to tell him or herself how to act in a given environment. It is "symbolic action toward the self, the symbolic activity the actor directs toward his or her self. It is active communication toward the self through the manipulation of symbols. . . . We think; we engage in minded behavior; we literally hold conversations with ourselves—yes, we constantly talk to ourselves, and we often answer to ourselves. "[59] All these take place in the endeavor to define the social objects around us before we use them to communicate with others.

The question of definition is a mind activity; and to point things to us implies that those things are meaningful to us. The mind defines the objects according to their use for us. To control overt actions, "people point things out to themselves as they walk down the street, or run or talk or

---

58. Ibid., 100; cf. Blumer, *Symbolic Interactionism*, 80.
59. Charon, *Symbolic Interactionism*, 98.

play."[60] In this case, human beings tell themselves about the things before they can use those things.

The ability to think is what probably distinguishes human beings from other animals that are thought to act 'intuitively' and without intention. They are not able to think reflectively, and in that sense, they are unable to have a symbolic communication. The complex brain of the human animal is able to think and dialogue within itself when exposed to the abstract symbol. Thinking is not without the activator; and in this case, language becomes the main activator of the human mind.

The Self

If the mind action or thinking involves having an inner dialogue within the individual him or herself, then it is important for us to understand what the self is. It should be made clear that the actor or individual acts both towards the social objects surrounding him or her and towards the self. When the individual acts towards the self, he or she is engaging in mind action. As Charon put it, when the individual engages him or herself in covert action (mind action) the self is an object to which he or she talks to. "It is active communication toward the self through the manipulation of symbols."[61]

Acting towards the self means taking the role of the other and seeing oneself in these roles. It is by making "oneself an object of oneself." Blumer points out that "One makes an object of oneself by addressing oneself from the standpoint of others."[62] This becomes possible through the

60. Ibid., 100.

61. Ibid, 98.

62. Blumer, *George Herbert Mead*, 58.

individual going out of him or herself and viewing him or herself from the outside.

Why Is Symbolic Interactionism an Important Perspective?

Perhaps one of the main reasons symbolic interaction has remained an important theoretical influence during most of the twentieth century is its attention to what actually occurs as human beings interact. It is empirical in its approach to reality. While the symbolic interaction perspective may seem to lack well-developed concepts, logical models, or theoretical rigor, as viewed by its critics, it makes up for this by studying social interactions of actual people in their social world. Given that it concerns human interaction, which is something any student of social sciences and the humanities is part of, the raw materials for the study of this interaction are available to anyone. At the same time, the study requires careful observation, an ability to pay attention to detail, and a consideration of the accepted and routine. While it may be difficult to understand the abstract ideas from the perspective of each sociologist, empirical study must move beyond the prejudice and bias of the observer.

In recent times, symbolic interactionism proves to be important even in biblical studies. The Bible itself is a symbol, which is full of more symbols inside it. The fact that the Bible has written words in it means those words need interpretation for us to understand what they really mean. Moreover, the Bible is full of names of places and of actions that have meanings. The Bible is also full of characters, the human-like figures interacting among themselves within the biblical stories. Symbolic interactionism helps

Bible readers ascertain the meaning of symbols used by the interacting figures, the meaning of the figures themselves as the Bible reader perceives them and the meaning of the face-to-face interaction that takes place in biblical stories. In this case, the perspective becomes helpful as meanings of biblical stories are mediated to current readers through the symbolically interacting characters.

In the following chapter I present one type of symbolic interaction that can also be seen in biblical texts: the dramaturgy. This type of symbolic interaction presents what happens when individual actors physically come into a face-to-face encounter with one another, the symbols they use, and the meaning they convey to each other in the interaction process. According to this type of symbolic interaction, communication is dramatic as each individual tries to impress another in the front stage. It is a play-like kind of communication whereby the world and what surrounds the actors is a stage where the drama is done. In this case, the next chapter will demonstrate what happens when interacting actors physically come into immediate presence with one another, which in turn will help understand the symbolic interaction in the texts within the gospel according to John.

Conclusion

The major concern of this chapter has been to examine the three major premises of the perspective of symbolic interactionism. It has examined the role of meaning in the process of interaction among social objects; the role of language, and human thinking or thought. It has been vivid in this chapter that human social interaction is important and cannot be taken for granted in most disciplines including biblical studies. This is mainly because the Bible itself is a symbol and the Bible is populated by symbols whose inter-actions need to be studied. Since the Bible is populated by symbols and the church that studies the Bible is also full of symbolic actions, therefore, the perspective of symbolic interactionism is as important to people as is water to fish.

THREE

Erving Goffman and Dramaturgy

Symbols shape what we buy, the television programs we choose
to enjoy, our responses to world events, our face-to-face
communications, even our sense of identity.

—GERALD ARBUCKLE, *CULTURE, INCULTURATION,*
AND THEOLOGIANS

Introduction

AFTER DISCUSSING THE VARIOUS theoretical dimensions of
the perspective in the previous chapter, this chapter briefly
surveys one of the applications of this perspective within
social sciences. One of the sociologists who used the perspective of symbolic interactionism to examine human interaction in social settings was Erving Goffman. Goffman
did not develop a theoretical approach that would explain
all parts of the social world, but he developed an analysis of
the interaction order—social situations, or "environments
in which two or more individuals are physically in one another's presence."[1] In the above preamble, Arbuckle states:

1. Lamert, *Goffman Reader*, 235.

"Symbols shape what we buy, the television programs we choose to enjoy, our responses to world events, our face-to-face communications, even our sense of identity."[2] These are the situations where we spend much or most of our life—in face-to-face activities involving others, whether these be everyday social situations, situations within organized structures (jobs, school), or unusual social situations (accidents, weddings, funerals). Goffman excels at observation, description, and insight, analyzing how people interpret and act in ordinary situations, and he provides guidelines concerning how to examine social situations.

Erving Goffman (1922–1982) was born and raised in Alberta, and attended the University of Toronto and the University of Chicago. He became a professor at Berkeley and later at the University of Pennsylvania. Goffman's best-known work is *The Presentation of the Self in Everyday Life*. This book employs the model of the theatre or theatrical performance as a means of analyzing how we develop and present ourselves to others. This approach is sometimes called dramaturgy and focuses on the techniques people use to convey impressions and create their selves. Dramaturgy comprises "the techniques/theory governing the composition of performance-as-text; . . . the set of techniques/theories governing the composition of sign/expressive means/actions which are woven together to create the texture of the performance, the performance text."[3] Moreover, performance text means "a complex network of different types of signs, expressive means, or actions, coming back to the etymology of the word 'text' which implies the idea of texture, of something woven together."[4] Goffman

2. Arbuckle, *Inculturation and the Theologians*, 19.

3. De Marinis, "Dramaturgy of the Spectator," 220.

4. Ibid., 219.

examines processes and procedures that are associated with social interactions in dramaturgical way. According to Goffman, it is these processes that build and maintain the social world.

In addition to the ordinary situations of everyday life, Goffman also examined unusual situations such as prisons and asylums, total institutions, using these to show how individuals used various means (many unauthorized) to maintain their sense of selfhood. He also used these settings to illustrate aspects of everyday life, and the unexamined assumptions we all make in the various situations and encounters in which we find ourselves. In this case, Goffman is credited for the introduction of the metaphor of life as theatre whereby all people are actors and the world we live in as a stage.

Dramaturgy and Everyday Life

A key to Goffman's dramaturgical analysis has to do with the physical encounter of an individual with other individuals in everyday life. A person cannot always stay alone. As a social being, a person has to interact with other people, even though interaction is not limited to physical encounters.[5] When it appears that individual has to interact with other people, and enter their immediate presence, such people will be interested to know information about who they are. The information they will seek to know will concern either what they do not know but would like to know, or the information they know and would like to share. Whether inquiring or sharing, the information will concern the whole sphere of human life: economic situation,

5. Cf. also Berger and Luckmann, *The Social Construction of Reality*, 23.

attitude, conception of self, competence, trustworthiness, and so on. The important question is why do people engage in this type of inquiry when an individual comes into their immediate physical presence? It may serve several purposes: it may enable them to determine the situation as it is presently and as the interaction continues. In defining the situation, people will align their acts according to the acts of the individual from whom they have inquired information.[6]

Some important things happen during the interaction when people have come into immediate physical presence to one another. But most of them are beyond what is happening. People want to know the attitudes, beliefs, feelings, etc. of an individual; yet, it is not easy to determine the "real" and the "true" information in the interaction. What each side (the side of the individual person and the side of the people with whom the individual interacts) does to the other is impression in order to convince that what it expresses is real and true. In this case, the individual will have to express oneself to others to impress them into believing what he or she expresses.[7] In fact this is the performance part demonstrated by the actors. This theatrical performance takes place on the front stage where the actors interact mostly face-to-face as a team or as individuals.

The expression both sides provide in order to impress is symbolic; it can be by the use of verbal symbols (words) or by symptomatic actions, actions the other side recognizes and identifies with the actor. Both of the two ways aim at conveying information about the actor. It is not necessary that only one way be used; it is possible that both ways can be used in a particular encounter. Does each side provide

6. Goffman, "Introduction," 97.
7. Ibid., 98.

real and true information as they use the ways? In most cases, it appears that individuals hardly provide "real" and "true" information as they talk or act towards others. This misinformation is mostly done intentionally. This means that the information provided on the front stage is likely to be different from the information provided backstage. The information provided on the front stage aims at impressing the other actors while the information backstage represents the real situation of the actor.

Dramaturgy and Impression Management

According to Goffman's analysis, it appears each side in the interaction will strive to convince the other side about the plausibility, truthfulness, and reality of what is communicated on the front stage. This means that each side will provide more promising information to the other side so that it can believe and accept, and hence provide a due response. This is called "impression management." Impression management entails care in controlling the kind of information shared in order to maintain the required impression. Goffman thus writes about the way a person with particular stigma controls information: "The issue is not that of managing tension generated during social contacts, but rather that of managing information about his failing. To display or not to display; to tell or not to tell; to let on or not to let on; to lie or not to lie; and in each case, to whom, how, when, and where."[8] However, in this dilemma, what is true and real remains hidden in the individual's self (beyond the interaction) and will be revealed when the individual leaves the presence of others.[9] This means what

8. Goffman, *Stigma*, 42.
9. Goffman, "Introduction," 98.

is real is at the backstage of the interaction; it is located in the individual's own self and is revealed at the absence of the interaction partner.

In providing promising information each side tries to influence the perception of the other side in order to fulfill a particular objective. In influencing the perception of another side, the communicator influences the receiver, especially in defining the situation. Since the purpose of the communicator is to influence the way the other side defines the situation, it will therefore communicate information that is of interest to it and conceal information that is of no interest to it.

Conclusion

This brief chapter concerned itself in describing what really happens when two individuals come into immediate presence in everyday life. One important aspect has been vivid: impression management. When two or more individuals interact each of them tries to convince the other party by controlling information. However, in this face-to-face dramaturgical interaction what is real mostly remains hidden in the individual's self.

Therefore, this chapter opens a door towards studying the symbolism of water in the gospel according to John. It provides necessary insight into how the characters in this gospel manage their impressions before other characters while controlling information they present before them.

FOUR

Interactionism and Symbolism of Water in the Gospel of John

The effect of symbolic action is emotionally experienced meaning. Signs are concerned about visible and quantifiable experience, but symbols seek to draw us beyond the observable to the higher experiential, transcendental level of knowledge.

—Gerald Arbuckle, *Culture, Inculturation, and Theologians*

Introduction

One of the great characteristics of the gospel of John is the interaction of characters. The gospel of John sets a stage of interaction whereby actors or characters use symbols to interact and convey meaning to the reader of the gospel. The narrator uses symbols to show how characters perceive each other's meanings, and communicate that meaning to the reader of the gospel. Moreover, the gospel portrays the stage where characters interact in a theatrical performance as they come into immediate presence to one another. There are various symbols in the gospel. Some of them are signs performed by Jesus in order to impress his audience; some of the acts are performed by the audience in order to impress Jesus; and other acts are done by actors in order to impress each other. This means that in reading the gospel of John one can easily note the difference between symbols and signs Jesus performed and the actions of characters done for the sake of impression. Hence, the characters' interactions are symbolic and dramaturgical because symbols are the major means of communication.

Symbols in the Gospel of John

The general meaning of symbols as social objects and the way symbolic interaction takes place has been covered in chapter two above. In this sub-section it is better to describe what a symbol is in relation to the gospel according to John and the difference between symbols and signs. This distinction between symbols and signs is important because the gospel of John is populated by signs of Jesus, which carry with them symbolic representations. Hence, though symbols are social objects, their definitions need to be revisited all the time.

We should understand at the outset that there are many studies of symbolism in John, but, as Schneiders puts it, "there do not seem to be any reliable or generally accepted criteria for the interpretation of symbols, any symbolic interpretation remains indemonstrable if not arbitrary." Since there is no single reliable meaning of symbol in the gospel according to John, the symbolism of water and the use of signs need not to have a single meaning. Their meanings need to be understood according to the contexts into which they appear. Hence, the multiplicity of meanings of symbols in the gospel of John exposes the reader to the vast meanings of symbols that characterize the interaction of characters.

Difference between a Sign and a Symbol in the Gospel of John

The difference between a symbol and a sign in the gospel of John is vivid in the way they stand for reality. Sandra M. Schneiders asserts that "A sign is something that stands for an absent reality. Its task is to refer the observer to something other than itself."[1] "A symbol, on the contrary, is the sensible expression of a present reality. Its task is to make the transcendent, or some aspects of the Transcendent, intersubjectively available and to mediate the participation of the observer in that which it reveals."[2] Schneiders provides the following examples to illustrate her point: "The human body is the primary symbol of the personality. Speech is a symbol of inner experience. Art symbolizes the beautiful. The church is the symbol of Christ. Most importantly, Jesus is the symbol of God."[3] In summary, therefore, "a symbol never stands for something. It is the sensible expression of the transcendent, that is, it is the locus of revelation (human or divine) and participation in that which is revealed."[4]

Arbuckle further notes: "Signs are concerned about visible and quantifiable experience, but symbols seek to draw us beyond the observable to the higher experiential,

1. Schneiders, "History and Symbolism," 372.
2. Ibid, cf. Jones, *The Symbol of Water*, 21.
3. Ibid.
4. Ibid.

transcendental level of knowledge."[5] Seth D. Kunin also states this difference: "A sign has a one-to-one correspondence with the object that it signifies. For example, a stop sign means stop and must be clear and unequivocal. A symbol, however, has a more complex with what it signifies. Rather than being one-to-one, it is multivocal; it evokes or brings together a complex set of diverse elements."[6] This implies that symbols are much broader in their spectrum as compared to signs.

As Schneiders, Arbuckle, and Kunin have pointed out above regarding the difference between a sign and a symbol, the symbolism presented in the fourth gospel places Jesus at the center of the whole symbolic interaction in the Johannine stage. Why should the narrator of the gospel of John place Jesus at the center of the entire symbolic interaction? This is mostly because Jesus himself is a symbol of God and of the glory of God; and that every other symbol in the gospel directs the interpreter towards understanding the identity of Jesus.[7] Being at the center of Johannine symbolism, Schneiders argues, "Jesus is the revelation of the Father. He is the sensible expression of the glory of God (1, 14)."[8] This is the revelatory part of the symbolic nature of Jesus. The second part is the mediatory dimension of the symbolic nature of Jesus. "Jesus is the locus of the disciples' participation in the glory of God. Jesus is the Temple where God and his people meet (2:19–21) and where true worship will be offered (4, 21–24). He is the way to the Father (14, 6). To be in the hand of Jesus is

---

5. Arbuckle, *Inculturation, and the Theologians*, 23.

6. Kunin, "Indigenous Traditions," 111.

7. Jones, *The Symbol of Water*, 24–25; cf. Schneiders, "History and Symbolism," 373.

8. Schneiders, "History and Symbolism," 373.

to be in the Father's hard (10, 28–29). To be possessed by Jesus is to belong to the Father (17, 10). To receive Jesus is to become a child of the Father (1, 12)."[9] In the above texts, Jesus represents the transcendent (heavenly); and it is through Jesus that the immanent (worldly) can know the transcendent.

One of the symbolic interactions portrayed in the gospel according to John is based upon the way the narrator of the gospel stories uses water as a symbol to communicate his message. It is common knowledge that life without water is inconceivable. A large percent of organisms live in water. Water is used for drinking, washing, and refreshment; it can also be a source of destruction of life. In this case, water has meaning depending on how it functions for human life; hence, water carries a symbol status because it is used in the gospel intentionally to communicate meaning.[10]

Division of the Gospel of John

Scholars have divided the gospel of John into several narrative blocks. I will illustrate only three of them. The first one is the old, traditional division of the gospel through which it is divided into four narrative blocks: the prologue (1:1–18), the Book of Signs (1:19—12:50), the Book of Glory (13:1—20:31), and the Epilogue (21:1–25).[11]

The second division is that of Mark W. G. Stibbe who divides the book into dramatic scenes. Stibbe arranges the dramatic scenes in the gospel of John following F. Hitchcock who claimed that in the gospel of John, "There is the

9. Ibid.

10. Koester, *Symbolism in the Gospel of John*, 155.

11. See for example Moloney and Harrington, *The Gospel of John*.

beginning, the development towards the central point, the central point, the development towards the end, the end."[12] This arrangement, according to Hitchcock, determines the plot of the gospel. Following this claim Stibbe arranges the dramatic scenes in the gospel that indicate the plot thus:

1. Chapter 1: This sets the first stage of the drama.

2. Chapters 2–4: These chapters describe the stage of the plot. Jesus begins his ministry journeying from Cana of Galilee to Jerusalem, through Samaria, then again to Cana.

3. Chapters 5–10: This is the second stage in the plot of the gospel. The narrative in these chapters develops towards the central point of the plot. Here the conflict of Jesus with Jewish authorities begin. The authorities plan to kill Jesus (see 5:19ff.) as Jesus continues with his ministry.

4. Chapters 11–12: This is the third stage of the plot. It is the central point of the plot. The miracle of raising Lazarus that Jesus performs provokes the authorities and causes the downfall of Jesus (11:45–53). From here, the Jewish council (the Sanhedrin) plotted to kill him (11:53).

5. Chapters 13–19: This is the fourth stage of the plot. It is the development towards the end. Jesus bids farewell to his disciples and is killed by the Jews. Stibbe asserts that "The seven chapters of the narrative cover the last twenty-four hours of Jesus life, from Thursday evening to Friday evening in Passover week."[13] Since for the Jews number seven indicated completeness or fulfillment, then the seven

12. Stibbe, *John's Gospel*, 35.

13. Ibid., 36.

chapters indicate that everything Jesus came for was completely fulfilled.

6. Chapter 20: This is the fifth and final stage of the plot of the gospel. It speaks about the resurrection of Jesus. This marks the end of the drama.

7. Chapter 21:1–25: This is the epilogue, trying to speak about the end (the resurrection of Jesus) and his appearance in Galilee.

The third division is that of Jones. Jones divides the gospel of John into four blocks:

1. The prologue (1:1–18): This opens the gospel and identifies the central character of the gospel.

2. The series of journeys of Jesus (1:19—17:26): Here we find the beginning of Jesus' ministry (1:19—3:36); the second journey to Jerusalem (4:1—5:47); the reminder of the middle portion of Jesus ministry (6:1—10:42); and the final journey to Jerusalem (11:1—17:26).

3. Jesus death (his "hour") and resurrection (18:1—20:31), and

4. The Epilogue (21:1–25): This recounts the post resurrection appearance of Jesus in Galilee.

I will closely follow Jones' logical arrangement in my presentation of the symbolism of water in the gospel of John. However, I will not provide full discussion of each block as I continue with my presentation, but discuss a little bit of the symbol of water as it appears in specific texts within the gospel.

The Symbolic Witness of John the Baptist (1:19–34)

The first scene of interaction in the Johannine symbolism of water is that of the witness of John the Baptist. From the first point of the verse we note a symbolic interaction. The narrator tells about the physical encounter between John, the witness of the heavenly being, and the representatives of the Jews, that is, the priests and the Levites. Their immediate presence results in the exchange of symbols as their means of communication. According to the narrator, the priests and Levites inquire of who John is (1:19). This question indicates that the Jews already had some idea of who John was. They had already interpreted him because John was a symbol to them. To them John represented something real, some thing present but not visible.

The response of John in this interaction reveals what the Jews had dialogued amongst themselves about. It reveals what they had back stage: John was the Christ, the Messiah. In fact, this was the way they defined John as a symbol before them. The reality of John not being the Messiah whom they expected becomes vivid as the interaction continues. John bears witness: "I am not the Christ." The representatives of the Jews redefine John: "What then? Are you Elijah?" John still rejects their redefinition: "I am not." They redefine him once more: "Are you the prophet?" He still rejects their redefinition, and they keep on inquiring him: "Who are you, that we may give an answer to those who sent us? What do you say about yourself?" John provides an answer about himself and his vocation: "I am the voice of one crying in the wilderness: 'Make straight the way of the LORD'" (1:19–23).

The whole of the above interaction is symbolic in the sense that there is an intentional use of symbols on both sides: the side of John the Baptist and the side of the priests and Levites as representatives of the Jews. The representative of the Jews interprets and re-interprets the symbols presented to them by John the Baptist and John the Baptist interprets the symbols used by his interaction partners. Since the core of their interaction was the acquisition of meaning in order to perceive of each other, then the interaction is symbolic interaction trying to understand the reality about John the Baptist.

On the one hand, John the Baptist tries to impress his interaction partners through his actions: his preaching, his baptism, and his systematic responses to their questions. On the other hand the priests and the Levites endeavor to impress John the Baptist through their questions and responses to him. In this case, each side of the interaction presents what needs to be known, information to be interpreted by the other side in the interaction order.

The major symbol mentioned by John the Baptist is water. The interpretation of the symbol brought by John the Baptist seems to be different from the one previously held by his interaction partners. The priests and the Levites understood that baptism was the work of the Anointed One and the prophets. The question of the priests and Levites to John the Baptist clearly indicates their symbolic interpretation of baptism: "They asked him, 'Then why are you baptizing, if you are neither the Christ, nor Elijah, nor the prophet?'" (John 1:25). John the Baptist tells the priests and the Levites some thing new about baptism, something different from what they prior understood as being the meaning of the baptismal symbol: "I baptize with water; but among you stands one whom you do not know, even he who comes after me, the thong of whose sandal I am not worthy to untie." (John 1:26).

As one reads verse twenty-six he or she encounters two symbolic representations mentioned by John the Baptist: "the one whom you do not know" and "he who comes after me." Who are these symbolic representations? Were these representations interpreted well by John the Baptist's interaction partners? How can the reader understand these representations? The text neither highlights what John the Baptist really meant nor the way his interlocutors interpreted such symbols. What John the Baptist emphasizes here is the symbolic significance of water as representative of the two other mentioned realities. For John the Baptist, therefore, water stands for things real but invisible. Water stands for the activities of "the one whom you do not know" and "he who comes after me."

Water appears for the first time in the gospel of John within this narrative. In this narrative, water is symbolically used as the source of purification, cleansing, or initiation. According to the Old Testament narratives, some aspects that made a person unclean and in need of purification include: associating with unclean creatures (Leviticus 11:25, 28, and 40), touching corpses of different kinds (Numbers 19:11–13), having skin diseases (see Leviticus 13:6, 34), rot in houses (Leviticus 14:47) or producing emissions from human sexual organs (Leviticus 15:5–33). These were removed through washing using water.[14] The right of baptism announced by John seems to be a common practice in the first century.[15] This was probably a proselyte baptism; but the way John presents baptism here aims at revealing Jesus to the Israelites. It is also possible to consider that the baptism announced by John was a precursor of the

---

14. Cf. Koester, *Symbolism in the Gospel of John*, 162.
15. Jones, *The Symbolism of Water*, 49.

following Christian baptism, even though it is not implied in the narrative.

However, the emphasis of the narrative is that there is something more to his baptism; there is something more and superior to what John was doing. It points to Jesus and his baptism with the Spirit not only for purification purposes as accorded by the first century ritual requirements, but it transcends that. The narrative points to the recognition of Jesus and his superiority in whatever John is doing because of what he will impart upon people through his baptism.[16] In the words of Jones, throughout the narrative "water does little more than signifying the arrival of something new."[17] Therefore, in the first narrative water represents the existing Jewish reality that people were to get there through it, while at the same time signifying the arrival of the new reality attained through the baptism of Jesus (by Spirit).

The Wedding Symbol in Cana (2:1–11)

This is the second time water appears in the gospel of John and is used symbolically to convey meaning to readers of the gospel. It appears at a specific scene, a scene of marriage celebration in Cana of Galilee. Jesus, his mother, and his disciples participate in the marriage banquet. John the Baptist who was involved in the symbolic interaction in the previous stage is no longer present. There are new actors in the scene. Actors interact symbolically, each participant aiming to impress the participants. The steward of the feast is there symbolically, including the wine, the six jars, and the wedding attendants. The wedding celebration

16. Ibid., 50.
17. Ibid., 51.

itself is a symbol that carries with it a special meaning. Despite the other symbols that cannot be discussed in this section, the symbolic representation of water is worth our attention here.

At this celebration, Jesus performs his first sign (remember all signs are symbols, but not all symbols are signs). He turns water into wine; the water is put into Jewish jars used for purification. The fact that disciples were ordered to fill the jars with water and then water becomes wine is itself a symbolic action. Look at the symbolic interaction in this scene: the actors are clearly placed, each with his or her own role to play. Language is the major symbol of communication among actors. In the scene, the first event is that "wine goes out." Wine itself is a symbol representing a certain reality; but it is "given out" and the need for more wine emerges. The second event emerges when the mother of Jesus reports to her son. The question is, why did the mother report to Jesus and not to the steward of the feast? Why did Jesus rebuke his mother for her reporting? Why did the mother of Jesus urge the disciples to do whatever Jesus commands? In other words, how did he know his son would command something valuable to be done? These questions and others not asked indicate the symbolic interaction among actors while each action carries with it meaning.

The third scene emerges when Jesus commands his disciples to fill in the six jars with water and take some water to the steward of the feast to test. And the fresh water changes into better wine than they had before. Some questions that illuminate the interaction order in this scene are: why were the six jars that were used for Jewish purification be filled with water, and not other vessels? Why water be filled in those jars and not any other liquid or material?

What does it mean by water changing into wine? Why did Jesus order his disciples to take the new wine from the water jars to the steward of the feast and not to any other people who were there?

Some scholars argue the water in this scene symbolizes the following: "'the re-creation of Jewish faith' through the ministry of Jesus, the perfecting and transforming of the Law by the gospel, and the replacement of the Jewish institutions by the salvation offered in Jesus."[18] Moreover, the fact that water in this event is associated with water jars, which were used for Jewish rites of purification (2:7, 9), means it is also possible that the narrative can have a symbolic representation of purification, probably a new purification, as the birth of a new people. It is possible that the water confirmed Jesus as Messiah, as foretold in the Law and Prophets.[19] In this case, the water certainly signifies that the Messianic age is present. This signification causes his disciples to believe in Jesus and what he does. This is because through the symbolic interaction of actors in the scene and the meaning of symbols used in the interaction order, the glory of Jesus is made visible to them.[20]

Symbolic Conversation of Jesus and Nicodemus (3:1–21)

After discussing the first sign with all its symbolic representations in the previous section, we now discuss the interaction between Jesus and Nicodemus and its symbolic representations. The whole of this narrative scene is occupied by two actors, who are both symbols representing a

18. Ibid., 63.
19. Koester, *Symbolism in the Gospel of John*, 162.
20. Cf. ibid.

particular reality. Jesus physically encounters Nicodemus, one of the prominent Pharisees and a Jewish leader; and Nicodemus physically encounters Jesus, a Jewish rabbi. Each of the actors in the interaction tries to impress the other actor through the communication of symbols (words) that convince the other actor. The first scene opens by Nicodemus coming to Jesus by night (not by noon time). This night is also a symbol that represents a particular reality. It should also be remembered that Pharisees claimed to know the truth but hardly fulfilled the requirements of that truth. Since Nicodemus was a Pharisee who belonged to the group that claimed to know the truth but hardly grasped it, night is possibly representative of this reality.

The second scene opens with the assertion of Nicodemus upon Jesus: "Rabbi, we know that you are a teacher [*sic*] come from God; for no one can do these signs that you do, unless God is with him" (John 3:2). This assertion indicates the way Nicodemus primarily understood Jesus as a symbol to him: a teacher from God who performs signs. Here Jesus does not respond to the assertion by answering "Yes I am the teacher from God." Rather, he adds more symbols for Nicodemus to interpret: "Truly, truly I say to you, unless one is born anew, he cannot see the Kingdom of God" (John 3:3). Two more symbols are added: to be born anew and the kingdom of God. The interaction order in the scene indicates the misinterpretations of Nicodemus of those symbols, which leads Jesus to further clarify. The story of the immediate physical encounter of Jesus with Nicodemus ends with Jesus speaking at length while the Pharisee (Nicodemus) fades silently. Water appears for the third time in the gospel of John, and appears only once in the whole story (3:5); yet, it embraces the efficacy of the whole story.

Again the interaction shows that language is the major symbol of communication between the two actors. Jesus emphasizes being "born *enothen*" being born of "water and Spirit" as opposed to "being born of flesh" (cf. John 3:5–6).[21] Here water most likely represents the new reality. "Being born of flesh" most likely represents the old reality; and being born of "water and Spirit" also represents the new reality. The way water is presented in the story shows that despite representing the new present reality, it also functions as the agent through which a person can reach or be incorporated in that new reality (cf. Jesus himself both represents God, and is the agent through whom people reach God).

To be born of water and Spirit, according to the interaction order presented in the Johannine stage, is most likely to enter into a new type of relationship, a relationship that is different from the old one. It is not only the matter of purification, but the access in the realm of God. "As the water turned into wine at Cana served as a means of seeing the glory of Jesus and as water of baptism made it possible for John the Baptist to identify the Lamb of God, so in this narrative water provides the means of believing in the realities and of accepting the truth proclaimed and manifested by Jesus."[22] In this story, therefore, "water symbolizes the separation of those who believe in and identify with Jesus from those who do not."[23] Water is symbolically

---

21. Some scholars that try to interpret the symbolic interaction of the actors in the story think that "being born of water" and "being born of Spirit" are different aspects. For such scholars, being born of water means a human birth of flesh and being born of Spirit is being born anew in the realm of God (see Schneiders, *Written that You May Believe*, 120).

22. Jones, *The Symbol of Water*, 75.

23. Ibid.

used to show the rite of passage through which one gains the sense of belonging to a particular group of people: people who believe and trust in the mere "teacher from God who performs signs" but the one who stands as a symbol of the most powerful God.

Symbolic Controversy over Baptism (3:22–30)

The narrative of Jesus' conversation with Nicodemus is intimately linked to the narrative of the controversy over baptism. In this narrative of the controversy over baptism Nicodemus—with whom Jesus had a dialogue about birth of water and Spirit—has disappeared. Jesus and his disciples reappear in Judea (3:22), but John and his disciples also reappear placed near Salim (3:23). These two groups are not in Jerusalem (3:23); but they are away from it. John and his disciples are joined by a Jew, whose name is not mentioned in the narrative.[24] However, both groups appear here as symbols to represent a particular reality.

The interaction order between Jesus and his disciples and John the Baptist and his disciples is displayed through the acts of each group that communicate meaning. In this narrative part, both Jesus and his disciples, and John and his disciples are engaged in the activity of baptizing people; John and his disciples are at Aenon near Salim in Shechem (3:23), and Jesus and his disciples at the land of Judea, just near Jerusalem (3:22). While John and his disciples conduct baptism quite away from Jerusalem (Aenon in Salim where there was plenty of water, a necessary element for his baptism), probably to the very north of it, Jesus and his disciples conduct it in Jerusalem, the very heart of Judaism

24. Ibid., 77.

and a place where water is scarce. This indicates that, despite the lack of enough water in Jerusalem, the baptism of Jesus and his disciples becomes more influential and stronger while that of John and his disciples diminishes and fades away despite having plenty of water in Aenon. The fading away of the baptism of John and the growth of the baptism of Jesus and his disciples is indicated by the flow of people to be baptized. Many people strikingly flow towards Jesus and his disciples to be baptized.[25] This most likely means that the amount of water was significant in the baptism of John (cf. the purification use of water by the Jewish rites required enough water); and it was less significant in the baptism of Jesus and his disciples, which signified the renewal of human faith. In this scene, therefore, the symbolic interactions of the two groups most likely indicate the transition between two significant eons: the Jewish and new Christian eons.

Jones also points out that only in this narrative "in the New Testament do we find evidence of a baptismal ministry conducted by Jesus."[26] On the one hand this assertion can provide evidence that Jesus conducted the sacrament; on the other hand, at the start of the narrative in chapter 4, the narrative about Jesus himself baptizing is corrected to indicate that only the disciples baptized (4:2) and not Jesus, as it was claimed in 3:2.[27] Despite the two arguments about Jesus' participation in the act of baptizing, the question remains open: did Jesus baptize as claimed by the supporter of the actual participation of Jesus; or did only the disciples baptize and not Jesus, as claimed by the

25. Jones, *The Symbol of Water*, 78; cf. Koester, *Symbolism in the Gospel of John*, 167.

26. Ibid., 78–79.

27. Ibid., 79.

narrator in 4:2? Whether Jesus baptized or his disciples did cannot be the issue of discussion here. Our main concern here is the symbolic representation of the controversy over baptism.

The baptism by Jesus and his disciples prompted controversy. A Jew (unnamed) was prompted to inform the disciples of John, and they in turn informed their teacher (John) about the resurgence of Jesus' ministry and that Jesus gained more disciples through his ministry. This indicates that Jesus conducted an extensive ministry in Judea near Jerusalem.[28] The questions that illuminate the interaction here are the following: what is the significance of the baptism of John and his disciples? What is the significance of the baptism of Jesus and his disciples? Why do both baptisms reappear simultaneously in this stage of interaction? Why does a controversy over baptism appear between the two actors in the scene? These questions illuminate the possible interaction order and the possible meaning of the actor's actions. The possible meaning of the controversy has already been stated. One baptism was preparatory (that of John) and the other a fulfillment (that of Jesus and his disciples). Therefore, it was implausible for both baptisms to continue. The presence of Jesus meant that John and his ministry should cease.

Symbolic Encounter of Jesus and the Samaritan Woman at Jacob's Well (John 4:1–42)

After looking at the role of water in baptism, the way Nicodemus interacts with Jesus and the major symbols they use, now we turn to examining the role of water towards

28. Ibid.

removing ethnic differences as indicated in the encounter of Jesus with the Samaritan woman at Jacob's well. In this narrative, Jesus has a physical, immediate encounter with a woman at the well named after Jacob (Jacob's well), one of the patriarchs. This story shows the first time Jesus meets a person who is not ethnically Jewish. Three important things happen in the encounter of Jesus with the woman: first, Jesus is in Samaria and has dealings with people there contrary to his Jewish ethical boundaries; second, he has conversation with a woman in a public space, a thing contrary to his Jewish and rabbinic status. Third, Jesus converses with a woman considered immoral by her community.[29] All the above issues place Jesus in a special place in relation to his fellow Jews. Jesus seems to deviate from the mainstream Jewish boundaries because he interacts contrary to the way he is supposed to interact as a Jew and as a Rabbi.

In order for us to understand the theme of water in this narrative, it is important we compare it to the previous narrative of Jesus' dialogue with Nicodemus. There are many similarities of the two narratives: first, both Nicodemus and the Samaritan woman converse with Jesus when the disciples are absent. This means that only two characters are involved in the conversation process. Second, both Nicodemus and the Samaritan woman were representatives of particular groups of people (the proud Jewish elites and the stigmatized and disregarded Samaritans, respectively). Third, water is mentioned as a central aspect of discussion in both narratives. Fourth, Jesus seems to have a similar attitude to both characters (to lead them towards the knowledge of him as the Messiah, evoke faith, and make them hold public confession of that faith).

29. Witherington III, *John's Wisdom*, 115.

Some of the differences between the two narratives are listed by Jones as follows:

> Unlike Nicodemus, a Jewish male privilege and standing, the woman was obviously, a Samaritan female, possibly of questionable integrity. In addition, Nicodemus was a rabbi where as the woman could have been forbidden to read Talmud. Nicodemus came to Jesus at night, but the woman met him in broad daylight. Nicodemus never quite understood what Jesus said to him and had progressively less to say in their conversation, whereas, although at times confused, seems at other points an equal in the dialogue. The meeting between Jesus and Nicodemus apparently remained a secret, but the woman left Jesus to go and tell others about him.[30]

From these differences, Jones concludes that Nicodemus is a symbol of "inability to accept Jesus," while "the woman of Samaria is a model of faith" in Jesus.[31] The symbolic use of water, especially the use of wells as meeting places is not only found in the gospel of John, it is also found in the Hebrew Bible (Old Testament). These events appear in the Hebrew Bible involving a "marriageable man and woman."[32] Jones lists some of these events as follows: "the meeting between Moses and the seven daughters of Midian (Exodus 2:15–22), the finding of a wife for Isaac from the woman who came to draw water at the well near Nahor (Genesis 24:10–61), a scene that has a striking number of verbal parallels with John 4, and, most interesting for this passage, the union of Jacob and the daughter of Laban

30. Jones, *The Symbol of Water*, 90.

31. Ibid.

32. Ibid., 91.

following an immediate physical encounter at the well (Genesis 29:1–30)."[33]

In these narratives from the Hebrew Bible, the future hero symbolically meets the future wife at the well. Theologians have provided the characteristics of a narrative whereby the future hero symbolically meets his future wife as follows: "First, a future bridegroom or his surrogate travels to a foreign land and, secondly, encounters a girl or a group of girls at a well. Thirdly, one of these characters draws water from the well. Fourthly, the girl or the group goes home to tell about the encounter with the stranger. Finally, a betrothal is arranged and concluded, usually following an invitation to a meal."[34]

This structure shows a symbolic interaction among characters with a specific meaning to readers. How then is the interaction among characters similar to the meeting between Jesus and the Samaritan woman at the well? As one can note, the meeting of Jesus with the woman has symbolic representation. Jesus himself represents a particular reality, and so does the woman in the interaction scene. The whole scene of interaction is also symbolic interaction in the sense that the acts are intentional. Jesus intentionally asks the woman to provide him some water. The woman intentionally responds to Jesus, challenging him about his different ethnic belonging. Moreover, the whole scene is full of language as a means of communication. Language as a symbol is something to be interpreted. Jesus speaks and the woman misinterprets, then Jesus clarifies. This shows us that language as a symbol is subject to interpretation. It carries meaning to the actor and is subject to interpretation by the person to whom the action

33. Ibid.
34. Ibid.

is directed. As it is in this scene, the interpretation of language as a symbol is not necessarily the same as intended by the actor. In this case, it becomes vivid that symbols are contextual and are understood contextually.

In this scene, the context of the Samaritans is not the same as that of the Jews, and this leads to the misunderstanding of language use. This misunderstanding happened in the previous scene when Jesus encountered Nicodemus. In both scenes, context becomes the great determinant for the way symbols are interpreted to yield meaning to the person to whom the action is directed.

Furthermore, the above episodes mentioned by Jones indicate a symbolic representation of a particular reality. A future hero symbolically meets the woman or women at the well. It should be kept in mind that Jesus, as a human being, was a "future hero." This understanding of Jesus makes this story have a number of similarities with stories in the Hebrew Bible. Jones provides the following insight regarding Jesus' encounter at the well:

> The narrative begins with an explanation of Jesus' decision to travel through Samaria, which, though not exactly foreign territory, was regarded by Jews as an 'alien' land (4:4). There he stops to rest at Jacob's well (4:6) where the woman quickly joins him (4:7) Although neither of them draws water from the well, Jesus requests water from the woman (4:7) and she requests water from him (4:15). Following these conversations, the woman returns to the village and tells the people about Jesus (4:28–29). The narrator mentions no meal and Jesus does not wed the woman, but the Samaritans do invite Jesus to stay with them (4:40) and, after two days,

> they, like the woman are united with him in faith
> (4:42).[35]

In the narrative of Jesus encountering the Samaritan woman at the well, the motif of water is one of the central features in the interaction scene. Jesus commands the woman to give him some water to drink soon after her arrival at the well. He commands the woman while aware that boundaries of relationship between Samaritans and Jews existed. By the year CE 65–66 the Jewish Council adopted a ruling that Samaritan women were constant menstruants from the cradle. The Jewish Council also affirmed that the worship practiced by the Samaritans at Mount Gerizim (Shechem) was not true worship of Yahweh but "filth."[36] Therefore, the interaction of Jesus with the woman of another ethnic group that was considered filthy indicates that he had a considerable intention.

It has been noted by scholars that both Jews and Samaritans believed water was an important element in their purification rites. This is because water or living water is central to the purity laws prescribed in both the Hebrew and Samaritan Bibles.[37] The two ethnic groups considered any "flowing" or "bubbling" water, for example, the one coming out of a natural spring or cistern, as "living water." The question of purification in the Samaritan and Jewish Scriptures appear in texts like Leviticus 14:5–6, 50–52 (for purifying skin diseases), Leviticus 15:13 (for purifying bodily discharges), and Numbers 19:17 (for purifying oneself from corpse defilements).[38] In this case, as Koester concludes, since water appears significant for purification

35. Ibid., 91–92.
36. Koester, *Symbolism in the Gospel of John*, 168.
37. Ibid.
38. Ibid.

of the two ethnic groups that were surrounded by many differences and misunderstandings, then "the living water imagery helps convey the idea that Jesus offered a gift that would remove the taint from the Samaritans [and the Jews] and lead to their inclusion in the [new] worshipping community."[39]

What is this "living water" that has been a great issue of discussion between Jesus and the woman in their interaction? The indicator of what this really is can be seen from the statement of Jesus in 4:13–14: "Whoever drinks of this water [from Jacob's well] will thirst again, but whoever drinks of the water I shall give him [living water] will never thirst; the water that I shall give will become in him a spring of water welling up to eternal life." Here again, as it was to the interaction between Jesus and Nicodemus, language becomes a symbol to convey a tangible message. Was this language understood by the woman? The narrative indicates that the Samaritan woman held a different interpretation from the one that was intended by Jesus.

Koester tries to provide the distinction between water from Jacob's well, which seems to be important for the woman and her community and the living water that Jesus provides. "The water in Jacob's well was bound to a place; it needed to be hauled out by hand, and it quenched thirst only for a short time. But the water Jesus promised was not bound to one place; it would spring up within a person so that he or she would never thirst again. The water from Jacob's well could extend life for a while, but living water from Jesus would issue into life everlasting, which in John's gospel refers to life lived in relationship with God."[40]

---

39. Ibid.

40. Koester, *Symbolism in the Gospel of John*, 169.

Moreover, Ben Witherington III sees Jesus as being both the source of "living water" and the living water itself. He contrasts between "normal water" and "living water" by pointing to the dichotomy between the Law (normal water) and Jesus as the Wisdom of God (living water). He points out that while the Torah (the Law) will still make its adherents thirst for more despite what it provides, the Wisdom of God (Jesus) provides lasting life and quenches people's thirst forever. In this aspect, Jesus himself is not only the source of living water, but, as the Wisdom of God, is the living water itself that quenches people's thirsts.[41]

We can conclude with Jones that, in the gospel of John, living water has the following possible symbolic representations: first, taking ideas from H. Odeberg, Jones writes that living water is a "symbol of the teaching and/or doctrine not of Judaism in general but of Jesus in particular."[42] The living water Jesus promises is a gift only he (Jesus) can provide; it is a gift from God offered to humanity through Jesus. It is both a teaching about spiritual life and eternal life itself. Living water provided by Jesus "represents a spiritual teaching that can become both the source of life and life itself."[43] The water Jesus provides is a teaching about spiritual reality and eternal life, and goes beyond the moralistic concerns of the Law, which the Jews and Samaritans considered their ultimate authority in their relationship with God.[44]

Second, taking ideas from Rudolf Bultmann, Jones asserts the living water Jesus promises is "a symbol of the revelation of Jesus or of the gift bestowed by that

41. Witherington III, *John's Wisdom*, 169.
42. Jones, *The Symbol of Water*, 111
43. Ibid.
44. Ibid.

revelation."[45] The words of Jesus to the woman, "If you knew the gift of God, and who it is that who is saying to you" point to himself and his ability to provide quenching water. Moreover, the fact that neither Jesus nor the woman drew water from the well in the whole interaction indicates that Jesus symbolically asked water from the woman in order to deliver his message to another ethnic group. In this case, living water symbolizes Jesus himself and what he is to offer to the world.

Third, the living water Jesus promises is "a symbol of the teaching and/or the revelation of Jesus and the Spirit which believers receive from Jesus and/or God."[46] In this aspect, the living water represents something spiritual that Jesus offers and not necessarily representing Jesus himself.

Fourth, living water represents "knowledge of Jesus and God." The narrative indicates the woman's development from ignorance about Jesus as the Messiah to acknowledging him as "the Saviour of the world" together with her Samaritan community. In this case, the gift of living water provided to them "yields the blessing of insight into Jesus' identity."[47]

Jones summarizes the possible representative symbolic role of water in the narrative as follows: "As water symbolically represented the means of revealing Jesus to Israel in the acts of John the Baptist (1:29–34), so too living water distinguishes Jesus as bearer of a gift from God (4:10). As the miracle performed with water manifested Jesus' glory to his disciples at the wedding at Cana (2:1–11), so also the discussion of living water prepares the woman for fuller understanding of his identity (4:26). As the

45. Ibid.
46. Ibid., 112.
47. Ibid.

dialogue with Nicodemus identifies water with the birth anew that provides entrance and access into eternal life (3:3–8), so also living water satisfies an immediate longing and becomes a source of life eternal."[48] In all these possible analogies, Jones indicates that the question of interpretation of symbolic use of language is crucial when people enter into interactions with actors in the interaction order.

Symbolic Healing of the Lame Man at the Pool (5:1–18)

The previous section dealt with the interaction of Jesus with the woman and her community. Jesus managed to impress the woman and her community. They believed him to be the Messiah and invited him to stay with them. In this section we indulge in the healing story and discuss the way symbolic interaction takes place among characters involved. Careful observation of the literary narrative indicates that there is a narrative transition from the end of chapter 4 to the beginning of chapter 5. The use of the words *meta tauta* and the mention of Jesus return to Jerusalem in the beginning of chapter 5 indicates that there is a change in time and place of his ministry. Jesus returns to Jerusalem where he participates in the feast of the Jews. Jesus does not return there as a stranger, but as a person who had been there before (cf. 2:13–22, 23–25, and 3:1–21).[49]

Jones divides the story of Jesus' encounter with the lame man into four scenes. The first scene is the introduction (5:1). The second scene is Jesus' encounter with the lame man (5:2–9) where there are several sub-narratives: a narrative about the pool and about the lame man (5:2–3,5);

48. Ibid., 113.
49. Ibid., 125.

the narrative about Jesus confronting the lame man (5:6); the narrative about the response of the lame man to Jesus' confrontation (5:7); and the narrative about the healing the lame man receives from Jesus (5:8–9). The third scene is the encounter of the Jews with the lame man (5:10–13). At this narrative part the man encounters questioning from the Jews: the Jews appear and initially question the man, and the man provides a response to them (5:10–11). The Jews are an important character in the gospel of John. In this narrative, the Jews appear for the first time within the gospel of John. They do not appear as a good character, but as an opposing and hostile character. They appear to oppose the "works" of Jesus in regard to the holy Sabbath. This is the main focus of their questioning. The man seems to violate the Sabbath by carrying his pallet.[50]

How does the man respond to the questioning of the Jews? The man immediately casts his blame upon Jesus who healed him, but he replied, "The man who made me well said to me, 'Pick up your mat and walk'" (John 5:11). On one hand, the man is right in his statement, because he just reported what was said to him by the one who healed him. Though he seems to cooperate with the Jews to a certain degree, he is innocent of what has happened because he emphasized not knowing the one who had healed him. On the other hand the man shows an irresponsibility to defend the one who healed him because he had that opportunity in the questioning process (cf. what the healed man did in John 9). The man does not show any interest in believing in the one who healed him, and neither does he show any sign of appreciating the act Jesus did for him.[51]

50. Ibid., 130.
51. Ibid.

Fourth, according to Jones, the narrative shows the Jews continue questioning the man in order to ascertain who healed him and the status of that person (5:12–13). The main problem with the Jews here is their concentration on the man's violation of the Sabbath rather than appreciating his healing, especially since he stayed in tribulation for thirty-eight years.[52] In this case, for the Jews, Sabbath observance seems to be more important than the life of the man.

Despite the man's irresponsibility to defend Jesus and the Jews' irresponsibility to appreciate what Jesus had done to the man, Jesus meets the man again at the temple and admonishes him about sin (5:14). Why does Jesus—who knows the man hasn't defended him before the Jews and that the Jews emphasized the sinfulness of the man's violation of the Sabbath—admonish the man about his sin? What sin does Jesus imply here? The one possible response to these questions is Jesus wanted to admonish the man for his lack of allegiance to him who made him whole through healing, and to identify him to the Jewish authorities after that. This is supported by the fact that Jesus admonishes the man not to sin just after the man identified Jesus as the one who healed him. Moreover, it is possible that Jesus thought it possible the man would side with authorities instead of believing in his healing power.[53]

Another possible response to the questions is that Jesus referred to the possible consequence of suffering as understood by the Jews of his time. He probably shared their Jewish understanding of sin. This is supported by the Jews' understanding of suffering as a consequence of one's sinfulness before God. However, none of the above responses

52. Ibid

53. Ibid., 131. Cf. Witherington III, *John's Wisdom*, 138–39.

are plausible because they lack convincing evidence from the narrative itself. Instead, the admonition of Jesus indicates there is a relationship between sin and moral consequences, and the man identifies Jesus before the Jews as the one who healed him. He sides with the Jewish authorities against Jesus even after the admonition (5:15), an act that leads to the persecution and increased desire of the Jews to put Jesus to death (5:16–18). Moreover, it is only in this admonition that the word "sin" appears in the narrative, and no discussion relates to this issue.

Symbolic Healing of the Man Born Blind (9:1–41)

Having surveyed the interaction order in the story of the lame man in the previous section, let us now turn to the story of the man born blind. The pool of Siloam stands as a symbol of life to the man born blind. The man, after obeying the command from Jesus to go and wash himself, he receives wholeness. The interaction between Jesus and the Pharisees, and between Jesus and the man born blind, centers on the pool of Siloam and its water. If the man was not healed after washing himself, the neighbors could not have been astonished and could not send the man to the Pharisees. Additionally, if the man was not healed the questioning of the Pharisees upon the man's parents (John 9:18–23) and upon the man himself could not have occurred. In this case, Jesus' healing activity could not have been recognized.

The healing encounter the man faces after washing himself indicates that water brings both controversy and life at the same time. The man's body is whole; but the work of Jesus is jeopardized by the Pharisees. Here water is at the same time a symbol of life and a symbol of death.[54] The man is enlightened after washing himself by the water, while the Pharisees are submerged in abject darkness because they fail to recognize the healing activity of water.

What I need to emphasize here is water stands as the point of departure for the whole symbolic interaction among characters. Jesus makes clay of the spittle and covers on the man's eyes (a symbol of blindness). The clay of the spittle comes from the earth (where the life of the man originated) and orders the man to go and wash himself in the water of Siloam. Water is the first dwelling place of the Spirit of God, which was blown into the man and the man became a living being. It is the place where the first life began before the man was created. The man removes the anointed clay of the spittle (a symbol of removing blindness) from his eyes. He is made whole. Therefore, the symbolic interaction enhanced by Jesus is based on promoting the life once enhanced by God.

The first interaction between the Pharisees and the man born blind is based on diminishing the life of the man. Through their arguments, they try to impress the man and the audience of other Jews to believe that what they try to defend is what is supposed to be held as the truth (John 9:13–17). The text so goes, "The Pharisee again asked him how he had received his sight. And he said to them, 'He put clay on my eyes, and I washed, and I see.' Some of the Pharisees said, 'This man is not from God for he does not

54. Water has always had both positive and negative meanings depending on the context and the situation of people. For example, Israelites see water as a source of salvation and life from the furious Pharaoh's army at the sea, while to Pharaoh's army and their chariots water is a symbol of doom. For Noah and his descendants water is a symbol of life while for the rest of the people water is a symbol of divine judgment. In 1 Peter 3:20 water of the flood stands as salvation while in 2 Peter 3:5–6 water is creation and judgment.

keep the Sabbath.'" The man is made whole after washing himself, but the Pharisees fail to recognize the activity of the life-giving water at Siloam. They direct their blames at Jesus who healed the man as a sinner because, according to them, he does not follow the law about the purity of the Sabbath and the teaching of the rabbis.[55] They want to know why he healed on the Sabbath. For them, Sabbath becomes more important than the life of the man born blind; and it stands as a yardstick to determine whether Jesus comes from God or not. In other words, the Pharisees value the vertical relationship more than the horizontal. They prefer to relate to God more than their fellow human being and their healing need.

In his second symbolic interaction between the Pharisees and the man born blind, the man receives more illumination after his healing and teaches them the truth while the Pharisees are blinded and see the man and Jesus as mere sinners. They want him to acknowledge the power of God as his creator, and they reject Jesus as his healer (John 9:24–34). It is here where the man tries to impress the Pharisees and the Jews and Jesus who healed him. The man who was ashamed and a beggar is now courageous, facing his Jewish leaders and trying to convince them to believe in Jesus who healed him by the water of Siloam. He convinces the Pharisees of the authority of Jesus and his divine origin. Jesus becomes the water of life that heals. However, the Pharisees are challenged by the enlightened man: "Do you also want to be his disciples?" (John 9:27). This question challenged their unwillingness to accept Jesus and his divine deeds. The man expected a negative answer from

55. See Malina and Rohrbauch, *Social-Science Commentary*, 173.

the Pharisees, his Jewish leaders.[56] In this story, the Pharisees do not understand what the man teaches because he belongs to a lower class and is not expected to teach them anything new. Likewise, the man leaves the Pharisees in darkness because they are of a higher class who pretend to understand what he teaches, but they don't.

In the end (John 9:35–41), Jesus comes along and reveals what entails his coming on earth. Here, the stage of interaction between Jesus and the Pharisees is opened. Jesus responds to the Pharisees' misunderstanding of the man's healing encounter. The text thus states the purpose of Jesus' coming on earth: "Jesus said, 'For judgment I came into this world, that those who do not see may see, and that those who see may become blind'" (John 9:39). The blind Pharisees opened their eyes to understand their blindness: "Some of the Pharisees near him heard this, and they said to him, 'Are we also blind?'" (John 9:40). Jesus leaves them to decide for themselves about their blindness. However, they remain unchanged despite their illumination. In this case, the story stands as the main symbol of the dichotomy between blindness and vision, and the role of water in making people whole through the activity of the Spirit of God who is the great illuminator.

Jesus' Symbolic Washing of His Disciples' Feet (John 13:1–20)

In the previous section we looked at the symbolic interaction of characters in the story of the man born blind. In this section we will discuss the way symbolic interaction manifests in the story of Jesus' washing the disciples' feet. The washing of feet is not a mere Johannine invention. It

56. Ibid., 171.

is a story that elucidates the existing Jewish tradition. The nature of the land that was inhabited by people and the weather exacerbated the existence of this tradition. The hot weather and the dusty land made the washing of feet one of the necessary aspects in the Jewish tradition. Washing of feet was done for several purposes: as preparation for meals and as a kind of hospitality to guests who entered one's house. Therefore, washing of feet was a symbol of welcome that served the purpose of cleanliness and comfort for people who were exposed to hot weather and dust.[57]

The activity of washing the feet of guests was not a pleasant one, and neither was it done by the guest's host. Since most of the hosts owned slaves, the duty of washing the feet of guests was either assigned to slaves, or the guests themselves did the washing of their own feet.[58]

However in the case of washing itself, it was unthinkable in this context that the superior person could do it to the inferior one. This means people who performed the washing were inferior ones. Even superior people like Abraham, who was known for hospitality, carried water to guests, treating them as social superiors to him (Gen 18:3–4). As one can note, Abraham's visitors were angelic beings who were social superiors to him.[59]

What then is the symbolic use of water in the event of Jesus' washing the feet of his disciples in John 13:1–20? In this text, the interacting characters are symbols themselves. Jesus is a symbol of the superiors in the Jewish society and the disciples are symbols of inferiors within the same society. Bauckham points out that "There can be no doubt that John understands the foot washing in relation to the cross,

57. Bauckham, *The Testimony*, 192.

58. Ibid.

59. Ibid., 193.

where the Jesus who in chapter 13 undertakes the role of a slave finally dies the death of a slave."[60] Bauckham further adds that "The foot washing both provides an interpretation of the meaning of the cross, as Jesus' self-humiliation and service for others, and also gains its own fullest meaning when seen in the light of the cross it prefigures."[61] Malina and Rohrbauch on their part believe foot washing is "a prophetic action that symbolizes forgiveness." As Jesus forgives the world, the disciples should forgive among themselves. This means Jesus moves from interaction between God and people towards people among themselves.[62]

In whatever way this text may be understood, it indicates a strong symbolic interaction among characters. Jesus, protagonist character and the supervisor, calls upon his disciples towards the washing process; the disciples, who are inferior, respond to Jesus' call; and Peter rejects the washing done by Jesus. Jesus utters thus towards him. "Unless I wash you, you have no share in me." This statement is a strong symbolic representation of the washing.

What does it mean to have a "share" in Christ that is depicted by Jesus' words? Despite Baulkham's symbolic meaning that concerns the soteriological significance of Jesus' humiliation, there are some other symbolic meanings that can be drawn from the interacting characters. Water is symbolically used as a social object of purification. Jesus represents the divine authority and the disciples stand for the worldly servants. Jesus purifies them for the missionary journey ahead of them, after Jesus ascended. This task of doing mission is clearly emphasized in the washing of

60. Ibid., 194.

61. Ibid.

62. Malina and Rohrbauch, *Social-Science Commentary*, 219–20.

feet that is done when the "hour" for Jesus to ascend has arrived.

Another possible meaning that can be drawn refers to the type of ministry the disciples are supposed to carry out. Since Abraham, the superior, washed the feet of the angelic beings making them social superiors to him, Jesus' ministry to be carried out by the disciples has to consider inferiors as social superiors. This view of service is proclaimed by Jesus, that whoever needs to be great among his disciples needs to be the least of all (see Matthew 18:1–5; Mark 9:33–37; Luke 9:46–48). In this proclamation, Jesus uses a child as a symbol of the inferior who is again made socially superior and an example to follow. In 1 Timothy 5:10, the washing of feet of houseguests becomes a symbolic activity to represent "good works" to widows. In this case Jesus uses the everyday activity of washing feet among the Jewish community in a symbolic way to explain a greater reality beyond the washing act itself. Jesus set to the disciples and to the church of the New Testament an example of service they should follow.

Conclusion

This chapter has examined more closely the way symbolic interaction is vividly used in the water narratives of the gospel according to John. It has used the theoretical perspectives of symbolic interactionism and dramaturgy of Erving Goffman to explain that symbolic interaction is not only limited to the everyday life of human beings, but is also present in the narratives in the Bible. The interaction of characters in the texts has shown that characters interact intentionally with the purpose of impressing one another. The meaning characters provide to interaction partners is not universal. It is contextually created by the characters themselves as they interact on the front stage. Moreover, it has been vivid in this chapter that Jesus and his deeds provide a remarkable example of interaction through which his disciples and the New Testament church needs to follow. Hence, the analysis of this chapter indicates more clearly the importance of communicating meaning among narrative characters and the possibility of reading biblical narratives by the use of social science perspectives, especially the perspective of symbolic interactionism.

FIVE

Conclusion

WE LIVE IN A world where symbols are as important as
life itself. Without symbols life can hardly be understood
because it is itself subject to definition. In other words, life
itself is a symbol with meaning. Symbols are vehicles of
what we need to communicate to other people and to our
own selves. This means that symbols, being the bases of
symbolic interaction among people, are what make people
creative and inspire them to live the life they live.

This book has shown that symbolic interactionism is
an important perspective not only in social sciences but
also in biblical studies. It has demonstrated that the biblical text, apart from the characters who populate it, is a
symbol with meaning in itself. The characters' interactions
are symbolic and intentional, each character struggling to
impress others. Impression management, as noted in the
various characters discussed in this book, is what keeps the
interaction going. Characters show to other characters that
which will convince them to believe they are good while
keeping the reality of what they are hidden. Moreover, each
character within the narratives uses symbols intentionally
in order to enhance communication and convey meaning.
In this case, in the interaction process what is real is invisible and what is visible is just physical appearance.

More specifically, this book discussed the symbolism of water as depicted in the gospel according to John. It started with the symbolism of water in the proclamation of John the Baptist who begins his ministry near the water of the river Jordan. The second water narrative is the wedding at Cana where Jesus and his disciples were invited and the way the change of water into wine becomes the center of interaction and the meaning of the story. This book moves to the other subsequent stories: the conversation of Jesus with Nicodemus, the controversy over baptism, the encounter of Jesus with the Samaritan woman, the healing of the lame man, the healing of the man born blind, and Jesus washing his disciples' feet are all symbolic actions that involve symbolic interactions of characters, each trying to impress the other characters. Through the survey of the perspective and its three premises in chapter 2, and the survey of the subsequent application within social sciences (by Erving Goffman) and in water narratives within John's gospel, this book has experimented in the possibility of using the social sciences in reading Scripture and discerning reality.

Bibliography

Arbuckle, Gerald A. *Culture, Inculturation and Theologians.* Collegeville, MN: Liturgical, 2010.

Bauckham, Richard. *The Testimony of the Beloved Disciple: Narrative, History, and Theology in the Gospel of John.* Grand Rapids: Baker Academic, 2007.

Berger, Peter, and Thomas Luckmann. *The Social Construction of Reality: A Treatise in the Sociology of Knowledge.* Garden City, NY: Doubleday, 1967.

Blumer, Herbert. *George Herbert Mead and Human Conduct.* Edited and introduced by Thomas J. Morrione. Walnut Creek, CA: AltaMira, 2004.

———. *Symbolic Interactionism: Perspective and Method.* Englewood Cliffs, NJ: Prentice Hall, 1969.

Charon, Joel M. *Symbolic Interactionism: An Introduction, An Interpretation, An Integration.* Fifth Edition. Upper Saddle River, NJ: Prentice Hall, 1995.

———. *Symbolic Interactionism: An Introduction, An Interpretation, An Integration.* Seventh Edition. Upper Saddle River, NJ: Prentice Hall, 2001.

Cohen, Anthony P. *Symbolic Construction of Community.* New York: Routledge, 1985.

De Marinis, Marco. "Dramaturgy of the Spectator." In *Performance: Critical Concepts in Literary and Cultural Studies,* edited by Philip Auslander, 219–35. Vol. 2. New York: Routledge, 2003.

Goffman, Erving. "Introduction in *The Presentation of Self in Everyday Life.*" In *Performance: Critical Concepts in Literary and Cultural Studies,* edited by Philip Auslander, 97–107. Vol. 1. New York: Routledge, 2003.

———. *Stigma: Notes on the Management of Spoiled Identity.* Englewood Cliffs, NJ: Prentice Hall, 1963.

Gätner, Bertil. *The Temple and the Community in the Qumran and the New Testament: A Comparative Study in the Temple Symbolism of the Qumran Texts and the New Testament.* Cambridge: Cambridge, University Press, 1965.

Griffin, Em. *A First Look at Communication Theory*. Third Edition. New York: McGraw Hill, 1997.

Herrick, James A. *The History and Theory of Rhetoric: An Introduction*. Third Edition. Allyn & Bacon, 2004.

Jones, Larry Paul. *The Symbol of Water in the Gospel of John*. Sheffield: Sheffield Academic, 1997.

Koester, Craig R. *Symbolism in the Gospel of John*. Minneapolis: Fortress, 1995.

Kunin, Seth D. "Indigenous Traditions and Anthropological Theory." In *A Companion to Religious Studies and Theology*, edited by Helen K. Bond, Seth D. Kunin, and Francesca Aran Murphy. Edinburgh: Edinburgh University Press, 2003.

Lamert, Charles, and Ann Branaman. *The Goffman Reader*. Oxford: Blackwell, 1997.

Malina, Bruce J., and Richard L. Rohrbauch. *Social-Science Commentary on the Gospel of John*. Minneapolis: Fortress, 1998.

Moloney, Francis J., and Daniel J. Harrington, editors. *The Gospel of John*. Sacra Pagina Series. Collegeville, MN: Liturgical, 1988.

Schneiders, Sandra M. "History and Symbolism in the Fourth Gospel." In *L'Evangile de Jean*. Gembloux: Leuven University Press, 1977.

———. *Written that You May Believe: Encountering Jesus in the Fourth Gospel*. New York: Crossroad, 1999.

Stibbe, Mark W. G. *John's Gospel*. New York: Routledge, 1994.

Tracy, David. *Plurality and Ambiguity: Hermeneutics, Religion, Hope*. London: SCM, 1987.

Witherington III, Ben. *John's Wisdom: A Commentary on the Fourth Gospel*. Louisville: Westminster John Knox, 1995.

www.ingramcontent.com/pod-product-compliance
Lightning Source LLC
Chambersburg PA
CBHW070515090426
42735CB00012B/2790